Praise for *Living Your Yoga*

"Judith Lasater's new book is a down-to-earth discussion of how we can use the age-old wisdom of yoga in order to reconnect with the sacred in everyday life."

—Georg Feuerstein, Ph.D., from the Preface
Founder-Director of the Yoga Research and Education Center

"Yes! *Living Your Yoga* is what it's all about. Here is a clear and friendly book that will help anyone embody the wisdom of yoga by consciously bringing it into daily life. The exercises are fun. They can help you learn how to do yoga all the time— now and now and now—when you are in the yoga room and when you are not. Take this book to heart."

—Erich Schiffmann
Author, *Yoga: The Spirit and Practice of Moving into Stillness*

"In this easy-to-read, inspiring book, Judith Lasater generously shares delightfully funny and poignant stories from her very American life, to show how we all can use the simple problems of daily living as a springboard for spiritual practice. Reading *Living Your Yoga* is like moving in with Lasater and her family for awhile. I enjoyed my visit immensely. She reminds us that yoga practice is primarily about mindfulness and is a twenty-four-hour-a-day activity. Take this book to bed, every night for a couple of months. Open it anywhere. Read a few pages. Reflect. Relax. Breathe. Smile. And have a good night's sleep."

—Beryl Bender Birch
Author, *Power Yoga*

D1005122

"In this delightful and practical book on yoga philosophy, Judith Lasater presents timeless wisdom with clarity and insight. She is a well-seasoned yogini, who writes from personal experience on how to use the events of daily life as yoga poses for the mind and the heart."

—Patricia Walden
Featured in *Yoga Journal's Yoga Practice for Beginners*

"Judith Lasater explains how her practice has helped her to sort through life's tangles, clarify her values, and renew her commitment to her ideals. She bares her soul so that we can see our own."

—Suza Francina, from the Foreword
Author, *The New Yoga for People Over 50*

"In her heartfelt and gently humorous manner, Judith Lasater shares her profound understanding of ancient yoga teachings, and translates the *Yoga Sutra* and *Bhagavad Gita* into a simple prescription for daily living. Whether you're a yoga student, yoga teacher, or yoga scholar, you'll be informed and inspired by *Living Your Yoga*."

—Kathryn Arnold
Editor in chief, *Yoga Journal*

Living Your Yoga

Also by Judith Lasater, Ph.D., P.T.

Relax and Renew: Restful Yoga for Stressful Times

Living Your Yoga

Finding the Spiritual in Everyday Life

Judith Lasater, Ph.D., P.T.

RODMELL PRESS
Berkeley, California
2000

Permissions and appreciations appear on page 153.

Printed in the United States of America

04 03 02 01 00   2 3 4 5 6 7 8

ISBN 0-9627138-8-0

Library of Congress Catalog Card Number: 99-75818

Editor
Linda Cogozzo

Copy Editor
Katherine L. Kaiser

Cover and Text Designer and Compositor
Jeanne M. Hendrickson, Hendrickson Design

Lithographer
McNaughton & Gunn, Inc.

Text set in Fairfield, Helvetica, and Papyrus

To the reader: The Sanskrit terms that appear throughout the text have been transliterated without the diacritical marks. The ṣ and ś have been written as sh.

For Rhoda, with love

Contents

Contents

PART THREE

Embracing All Life: Yoga in the World

Acknowledgments

This book reflects a personal journey that began decades ago. I have had important helpers along the way. I thank each of you for your support.

First, I thank my family, specifically my husband, Ike, and our three children, Miles, Kam, and Elizabeth. Their insights about life, as well as their sometimes pungent comments on how I am missing the essential truth of any given moment, have been invaluable and fill this book.

Next, I acknowledge and thank my yoga students, especially those who have stuck with me for many years. Having the responsibility of teaching has inspired me to practice and to continue to learn.

Finally, I thank Linda Cogozzo and Donald Moyer of Rodmell Press, who have consistently supported me during the dark times and celebrated with me during the happy ones.

Foreword

In *Living Your Yoga,* Judith Lasater provides an elegant yet sturdy bridge between yoga on the mat and the yoga of daily life. When we leave the sanctuary of a yoga studio, roll up our sleeves, and set to work in the world, we must be careful not to add to the confusion and violence that already exist. This book of essays and guided practices, based on selected verses from the *Yoga Sutra* and the *Bhagavad Gita,* can assist us in this endeavor.

The author shares her understanding of yoga's ancient teachings and shows us how to apply them to our contemporary lives. Especially insightful is the warm and personal way in which she addresses the division many of us feel when the peace we experience in our yoga practice is disrupted by everyday reality. Judith Lasater explains how her practice has helped her to sort through life's tangles, clarify her values, and renew her commitment to her ideals. She bares her soul so that we can see our own.

Now that yoga has entered the mainstream, it is more important than ever for yoga teachers to communicate how postures, breathing techniques, and meditation are rooted in moral principles. Yoga addresses the ethical life through a whole range of practices that encourages us to live in harmony with nature, making our actions conducive to both personal and planetary health. The great yoga teachers urge us to consider all aspects of our lives, to revere all living things, and to take no more than we need. Surely, a complete yoga practice must encompass a way of life that addresses the harm we inflict on ourselves and other living things, as well as doing our part to reduce pollution and to share the limited resources of our planet fairly with all other beings. In *Living Your Yoga,* Judith Lasater shows herself to be a part of this teaching lineage.

I am thankful every day for the great gift of yoga. The precious time I spend practicing yoga's healing postures provides me with a much-needed physical and psychological cleansing. Yoga gives me a sense of peace and expansion; equally important, it gives me the inner strength and resiliency needed to face the complexities of life in the twenty-first century.

Judith Lasater has helped me to understand more of yoga's universal truths and to use them conscientiously in my life. Her helpful, accessible book will introduce many more people to yoga's timeless wisdom. Yoga teachers and students everywhere will be inspired to deepen their understanding of yoga philosophy. *Living Your Yoga* is a book I will recommend wholeheartedly to my students in the years to come.

Suza Francina
Author, *The New Yoga for People Over 50*
Ojai, California
September 1999

Preface

The complex five-thousand-year-old tradition of yoga is about a very simple thing: happiness (*ananda*). Yoga tells us that in order to realize lasting happiness, we must discover our true, spiritual nature. This requires that we commit ourselves to nothing less than self-transformation and self-transcendence. For although our true nature, or spiritual Self, is always the same, it tends to be obscured by our conventional thoughts, emotions, and patterns of behavior. The yoga tradition compares this circumstance to the brightly shining sun, which is ever radiant but periodically hidden from our view by drifting dark clouds.

Yoga helps us to remove all obstructing (mental) clouds, so that we may come to enjoy the sunshine within. It is an extensive program of reeducation through which we learn, step by step, to live in the light of our true nature. Only when we have truly found ourselves will we be able to live in peace, harmony, and happiness in the world. This is what is sometimes called the sacred life.

Judith Lasater's new book is a down-to-earth discussion of how we can use the age-old wisdom of yoga in order to reconnect with the sacred in everyday life. For many people, practicing yoga means to do yoga postures once or twice a week, or even every day. Although this approach can yield many benefits, such as better health and greater vitality, the real power of yoga is unleashed only when we engage yoga as a way of life, twenty-four hours a day. Yoga is universal and applicable in all situations. It is first and foremost a mental, or inner, discipline. Even its physical postures *(asana)* have a spiritual purpose and must be practiced with full awareness. Every single yoga technique—from postures to cleansing practices to meditation—is a tool for discovering the abiding happiness of the ultimate Self, or Spirit. In *Living Your Yoga,* the author, who has been practicing yoga since 1970, shares with readers her own experiences on the always bumpy road to self-discovery. Her honesty is commendable, for some of her disclosures are unflattering but characterize the experience of most of us: Whenever we step into the light, our shadow side also becomes more apparent. Working with our psychological shadow is a necessary task if we want to integrate our spiritual values and goals—and thus our yoga practice—into the rest of our lives.

The path toward yoga's lofty goal of Self-realization *(atma-jnana)* is not in the least glamorous. On the contrary, it is quite humbling. For we must constantly, bravely, and compassionately face our limitations in order to realize our unlimited potential as spiritual beings. Judith Lasater, speaking from her own experience, points the way for other Westerners who are eager to apply the immense wisdom of yoga to their everyday lives. I can wholeheartedly recommend this book, which combines a clear vision with invaluable practical insights forged in the fire of the author's day-to-day yogic practice.

Georg Feuerstein, Ph.D.
Founder-Director of the Yoga Research and Education Center
Oakland, California
October 1999

Introduction

Living Your Yoga is about finding the spiritual in everyday life. I started practicing *asana*, or "yoga poses," in 1970 and began teaching them in 1971. Throughout the years, I have continued to learn about myself through these poses. For example, when I was in labor with my first child, I thought of each contraction as a pose. I focused on my breath and on letting go, just as in a challenging asana. After my son was born, I wished that I could bring what I learned in asana not only into birthing, but also more consciously into my parenting, my marriage, my friendships, and my work. I continued to study yoga philosophy and began to explore ways to actualize these teachings in the circumstances of my daily life. I found this to be of great value and, in 1981, began to share my exploration in my teaching. Initially, I began some of my classes and workshops with a discussion of an aphorism from Patanjali's *Yoga Sutra*. In 1988, I began teaching asana workshops that focused on life as practice. I called these workshops "Living Your Yoga." This book is the result of my ongoing personal exploration, my work with my students and colleagues, and my interactions with my family, friends, and the world around me.

Longing for the Sacred

Yoga has become an integral part of modern Western society. In an era of increasingly sophisticated technology, this centuries-old art and philosophy has ever-increasing appeal. In fact, a 1999 *Yoga Journal* study estimates that in the United States alone, more than ten million people actively practice yoga.[1]

Yoga's resurgence of popularity is a reflection of our urge to reconnect with the sacred. Most of us don't often engage in the rituals associated with worship since ancient times: we rarely sing or dance or pray. For centuries these had been a sacred context within which we connected with ourselves, one another, and the Divine. But why not turn toward the religious traditions of our childhoods? Why pick one from a far-away land that most of us will never visit?

It has been my experience that many religious traditions stress developing a relationship with an external deity. Worship is something you *do,* not something you *are.* For example, I grew up going to church two times on Sunday, as well as on Wednesday nights. I always felt that God was a very distant being who, paradoxically, was interested in even the smallest of my sins. I wanted more: a direct and personal relationship with the Divine.

I started yoga in my early twenties. I was studying dance and had developed arthritis. I heard that yoga's gentle stretching and relaxation techniques could help me. I originally planned to resume dance classes and performing after my arthritis had improved. Because I loved movement and expressed myself through it, I was ecstatic after my first yoga class. I had been taught to worship by praying or singing. But here was a philosophy that accepted the potential of human movement as sacred and worshipful—all in this very moment, here on Earth.

What I now know is that I had been seeking wholeness through integration of my body, my mind, and my spirit. Whether consciously or unconsciously, we all search for answers to the fundamental questions of life. As children, we ask "Who am I?," "Why am I?," and "Where am I?" When my son was seven years old, he came down the stairs one morning and, as if in midconversation with me, asked, "But who made God?" As adults, we know that although we may worship or practice with others, the process of spiritual understanding and growth goes on separately in each of us. I was raised in Texas, and I can still hear my mother's homily: "Honey, everybody has to hoe their own row." We are left with trying to understand the mystery of life with our own hearts and own minds. With yoga, Indian sages have given us a way to understand the nature of reality.

The word *yoga* comes from Sanskrit, the scriptural language of ancient India. Its root is the verb *yuj,* meaning "to yoke" or "to unite." Yoga is actually two things. First, it is a state of being in which the individual practitioner experiences a cellular connection with that which is the Universe, the Source, or God. This state is sometimes described by athletes as "being in the zone." For *yogis,* or "yoga practitioners," this is *samadhi.* Contrary to popular belief, samadhi is not a trance: in fact, it is the opposite. It is a state in which we experience total clarity of awareness. But for most of us, samadhi does not seem relevant to our daily lives. Here is where the second aspect of yoga—the practices associated with that deeply connected state of being—comes in. Most of us have heard of yoga's poses, its *pranayama,* or "breathing exercises," and its meditation techniques. Less known is the fact that these practices are rooted in a moral code that is the very foundation of yoga. This moral code is made up of *yama* ("restraints") and *niyama* ("observances"). The yamas are nonviolence, truth, nonstealing, clarity about sexual activity, and nongreed; the niyamas are purity, contentment, consistency, study, and devotion.[2] Although we may enjoy our personal yoga practice or classes, it is only when we make yoga's foundation a part of our daily lives that we will be transformed.

It is important to understand what transformation means in relationship to your inner life. At first blush, it would seem that transformation is about changing. However, it does not mean that you use yoga to change into something different. Rather, yoga takes you *back* to your true Self. The practice of "living your yoga" uses the psychology of yoga to uncover this Self, or what yoga calls *atman*. To do this, you must understand what it means to practice.

Practicing to Live, Living to Practice

Many of us have a negative reaction to the word *practice,* probably because it reminds us of being coerced into piano lessons or some other detested activity in childhood. For me, *practice* has a different meaning. It is the consistent willingness to open to life in all of its joy and pain. This definition certainly includes what you have always thought of as your yoga practice, such as poses, breathing exercises, and meditation. But it also casts a wider net to encompass frustration with your temperamental car, the argument you had with your friend, washing your dinner dishes, and your apprehension about an important meeting. In other words, to practice is to pay attention to your whole life: your thoughts, your bodily sensations, and your speech and other actions. As you do, you will discover that nothing is separate from anything else. Thoughts are the sensations of the mind just as sensations are the thoughts of the body. Each moment of your life is a moment of potential practice.

Practice, then, can be understood as a willingness to return to the reality of this very moment, that is, to observe with dispassion and clarity exactly what is—right now. Does this moment call for silence or for answers? Is the person in front of me asking for information or the reassurance of my love? Am I reacting from fear or from necessity? Obviously, there is no guarantee that I am correct. But relying on paying attention to the thoughts and sensations of the moment will give me a chance to respond to life less from my patterns of defense and more from integrity.

A point of clarification: Practicing being present with all the moments of your life does not mean that everything that happens is okay and that you just have to learn to accept it. Things happen in the world that are harmful and even horrific. The practice of being fully present may even move you to dedicate your life to changing the suffering you see in the world. I am not asking you to change into something you think is better or more spiritual. I am asking you to consider removing the layers of doubt, fear, and denial that keep you from experiencing connection with your own wholeness. One way to do this is to garner inspiration from the teachers and practitioners who have paved the way.

Ancient Texts, Modern Lives

In our fast-moving world, the emphasis is on the latest events, the newest scientific discovery, and the hottest fashion. Yet yoga's ancient texts still offer us important and relevant insights into how to live well. One of the most important is the *Yoga Sutra,* compiled in perhaps 200 B.C.E., although scholars debate this date. The author of the *Yoga Sutra,* Patanjali is generally thought to have been a physician, Sanskrit scholar, grammarian, and yogi. Each *sutra,* or "thread," is a terse phrase. As such, it is an ideal construct for memorizing sacred teachings. The *Yoga Sutra* is divided into four *pada,* or "books," that explain the nature of higher consciousness, the practices of yoga, the supernormal powers that can come from practice, and the state of final liberation. The second book in particular offers interesting and powerful insights into the workings of the mind and the obstacles to wholeness. Many chapters in *Living Your Yoga* will be based on concepts drawn directly from the *Yoga Sutra.*

Another source of inspiration is the *Bhagavad Gita,* or "Song of God," part of a larger work called the *Mahabharata.* Written in approximately the third or fourth century B.C.E. and consisting of seven hundred stanzas, it takes the form of a dialogue between Krishna, a manifestation of the god Vishnu, and Arjuna, a young man from a good family who is in the midst of a spiritual crisis. This upheaval takes place on a battlefield, where Arjuna must fight and possibly kill some of his own relatives. Their dialogue is a metaphor for the struggle we must all face between our attachments and our clarity. Throughout, Krishna advises

Arjuna to fight the good fight, to continue to live with courage, and to accept the challenges that life presents. Some of the chapters in *Living Your Yoga* draw from the wisdom of the *Bhagavad Gita*.

About This Book

Living Your Yoga is divided into three parts, each exploring the nitty-gritty of those qualities to be cultivated and those qualities to be transformed through awareness. Part One, "Awakening Awareness: Yoga within Yourself," has seven chapters: "Spiritual Seeking," "Discipline," "Letting Go," "Self-Judgment," "Faith," "Perspective," and "Courage." A crucial and perhaps most powerful aspect of your relationship with yourself is your internal dialogue. This is true for at least three reasons. First, how you talk to yourself reflects your thinking, which may not be truly reflective of reality. Second, it may be repeated for years, thus becoming embedded in your consciousness. Finally, it exists in the silence of your mind, unchallenged by the thoughts and insights of others. In this section, I suggest various ways to cultivate awareness of this inner dialogue and relax its hold on your consciousness.

Part Two, "Widening the Circle: Yoga and Relationships," addresses how to become more loving with your partner, your children, your family, and your friends. Because this love can spring only from your own internal clarity, this section comes second. It also has seven chapters: "Compassion," "Control," "Fear," "Patience," "Attachment and Aversion," "Suffering," and "Impermanence." Like most of us, I have found few things more challenging in life than learning to remain truly open and aware in intimate relationships. I like to say that I have several gurus, and they share my last name!

Part Three, "Embracing All Life: Yoga in the World," has seven chapters: "Greed," "Service," "Connection," "Truth," "Success," "Nonviolence," and "Love." You encounter a challenging level of practice when you venture beyond the boundaries of family and friends. How do you practice when the environment does not support you or is even openly hostile? It would be easy to separate yourself from those who you decide are not on "the path." If you relax your view, you may see that it is all one path and that we are all on it.

Each chapter has five parts: a verse from the *Yoga Sutra* or the *Bhagavad Gita,* an essay, a guided practice, more suggestions for practice, and Mantras for Daily Living. The practice sections are intended to support your exploration of living your yoga. Some will be on your yoga mat; others will be off it. *Mantra* comes from the Sanskrit words *manas* (which means "mind") and *tra* (which means "to transcend"). A mantra is something that helps you to transcend ordinary ways of thinking. These are meant to be your life-affirming companions throughout the day. You might say that each is a modern-day sutra.

It is my hope you will find comfort in the essays, and that you will return to the practices and mantras again and again. If you are so inspired, design practices and write mantras of your own. To develop a greater intimacy with the *Yoga Sutra* and the *Bhagavad Gita,* you can recite or chant their verses at the beginning or end (or both) of your practice or any of your daily activities. As Dag Hammarskjöld, secretary general to the United Nations (1953–61), writes in *Markings*, "In our era, the road to holiness necessarily passes through the world of action."[3] Use this book in whatever ways best serve your needs. *Living Your Yoga* is my gift to you.

PART ONE

Awakening Awareness: Yoga within Yourself

1

Spiritual Seeking

tada drashtuh sva-rupe'vasthanam
Then the seer abides in its essence.
—*Yoga Sutra* 1:3

Some years ago, I was working at my desk and realized that I had misplaced a bill that was due. While I anxiously searched for it, my then four-year-old daughter came into the room and asked for my attention. I said that I was busy looking for something important and to come back later. In a few minutes she returned and asked quietly, "Have you found yourself yet, Mommy?" I was humbled by her question. Had I found myself or anything else after years of yoga study and spiritual seeking? I had, but the "path" was not what I had imagined at the beginning of my journey in 1970.

At the outset, I believed that to be spiritual meant that I had to seek, find, and accomplish something outside of myself that would bring me happiness and fulfillment. For example, I sought the company of well-known gurus and teachers, because I was convinced that they had the answers. I practiced a rigid program of yoga poses, holding them for excruciatingly long periods of time in hopes of self-transformation. And I read every book on yoga and enlightenment that I could find.

I thought that I understood what it meant to be a spiritual person until the day when I became angrier than I had ever been in my life because of a disagreement with an employee. I literally saw red. I found out that this is not a metaphor but an actual physiological phenomenon. In that flash, I understood how someone could murder in the heat of the moment. I was shocked by the depth of my anger and retreated to my room, where I sat in despair. After all my years of yoga practice, how could I become so incredibly angry? I felt that I was a failure, and that all of my attempts to reach a higher level of spiritual development were a joke. I could feel my ideas about myself as a spiritual person draining out of me. At exactly the same moment, something else was filling me up. It was a feeling, an understanding, an experience made up of equal parts equanimity and peace. This state lasted for three days, during which I needed almost no food or sleep. I could see clearly that it was not my ideas about spirituality that would bring peace to my life. Whether we seek something called spirituality, holiness, or enlightenment, the route to it is through our humanness, complete with our strengths *and* our weaknesses, our successes *and* our failures. You might say that we use ourselves to discover ourselves. In my case, it required a deep letting go of what I *thought* that enlightenment might be that allowed me the smallest taste of it.

Many great teachers have pointed the way, emphasizing that they (and their teachings), in and of themselves, are not the answer. For example, Jesus said, "The kingdom of God is within you" (Luke 17:21). Patanjali addresses this same point in the first book, verse three, of his *Yoga Sutra: tada drashtuh sva-rupe'vasthanam,* or "Then the seer abides in its essence."[1] This important verse clarifies a core concept of Patanjali's work. He begins with *tada,* meaning "then" or "when one is in the state of yoga."[2] (It should be noted that Patanjali uses *yoga* to mean "a state of wholeness" as well as the practices associated with this state.[3]) And when you are in a state of yoga, or wholeness, you rest in your own true nature.

A favorite image I use to explain this verse to my students is that of a sculptor. When carving stone, the sculptor removes everything that is *not* the statue. She does not add anything to create it, except the willingness to do the work. The art of revealing beauty lies in removing what conceals it. So, too, Patanjali tells us that wholeness exists within us. Our work is to chisel away at everything that is not essence, not Self.

Many of us come to yoga because of some difficulty in our lives. For some, it is physical, such as lower back or knee discomfort. For others, it is emotional, such as depression. And for still others, the draw is philosophical, such as feeling that life lacks meaning. Most of us have a combination of reasons. However, often the dawning of yoga is coupled with an outwardly acknowledged or inwardly unexpressed expectation that yoga can solve problems, eliminate pain, and, most important, guarantee us that they will not recur. As I discovered through my experience with anger, nothing could be further from the truth.

Although yoga practice certainly can help our aching backs and bolster our spirits, it cannot insulate us from the pain that life inevitably brings, such as losing loved ones, illness, aging, not getting what we want—or even getting what we want. If yoga does not ensure a life without pain, then why do it? I have found that being in "a state of yoga" relieves *suffering,* specifically the suffering caused by being in separation from my wholeness.

Suffering differs from pain. Suffering is caused by the emotional reaction we lay on top of our pain. By becoming aware of our emotions and thoughts about pain, their hold on us can be released and our suffering can be lessened. The avenue to this awareness is through constant attention, remembering that each moment is holy and holds the potential for self-transformation. This awareness is the *tada,* or "state of yoga," about which Patanjali speaks.

From this perspective, spiritual seeking is not what we do outwardly, but what we acknowledge inwardly. To practice yoga in the deepest sense is to commit to developing awareness by observing our lives: our thoughts, our words, and our actions. There are many yoga techniques that can support us along the way, such as yoga poses, breathing practices, and meditation. But these are not ends in themselves, but means to the Self. The real beginning of spiritual practice is evident when we accept responsibility for ourselves, that is, when we acknowledge that ultimately there are no answers outside of ourselves, and no gurus, no teachers, and no philosophies that can solve the problems of our lives. They can only suggest, guide, and inspire. It is our dedication to living with open hearts and our commitment to the day-to-day details of our lives that will transform us. When we are open to the present moment, we shine forth. At these times, we are not *on* a spiritual path: we *are* the spiritual path.

Abiding Practice

We begin with Abiding Practice. If there really are no answers outside of ourselves, then we must learn to turn toward ourselves and be comfortable in doing so. Abiding Practice can remind us that there is nothing we need to be whole that does not already exist within us. It combines a yoga pose with a Mantra for Daily Living. You can select a mantra from those that follow, one from another chapter, or you can create one of your own. Abiding Practice can be done practically anywhere, anytime. Set aside some time each day for practice, even if it is only five minutes. Above all, be kind to yourself. Do what you can: never force anything.

To begin, select a quiet space at home or work. Decide how much time you have, and set a timer so you do not have to watch the clock during practice. Choose a soothing yoga pose in which you are comfortable, such as lying in Basic Relaxation Pose (*Shavasana*) in your yoga practice space or on your bed, or Seated Mountain Pose (*Tadasana,* variation) at work. Make yourself comfortable. For example, you can place a rolled blanket under your knees and a rolled towel under your neck in Basic Relaxation Pose, or a stack of books under your feet and a rolled towel at your lumbar spine for support in Seated Mountain Pose. Whichever you choose, make sure that your body is placed in a symmetrical position, and that your spine is soft and long.

Once in position, close your eyes, allowing them to look downward toward your heart. If you are lying down, cover your eyes with a wash cloth. Relax your jaw and throat. Spend the next few minutes gently observing your breath.

When you feel settled, say your Mantra for Daily Living to yourself. Rest in the pose.

Most daily activities are goal oriented. In Abiding Practice, there is no objective except to fully experience your own life, free of the distraction caused by thoughts, plans, and even by moving around. We all spend most of our time forgetting to feel, to sense, and to know life—moment by moment. Abiding Practice helps you to experience each moment completely. Instead of trying to fill yourself up, this is the your chance to feel empty, feel still, and feel present.

To end practice, follow the rise and fall of the breath as you did at the beginning of the exercise, and repeat your Mantra for Daily Living. When you feel complete, open your eyes and come out of the pose. Stretch and take the time you need to make the transition to your next activity, knowing that all is well within you.

Other Practice Suggestions

- Create a sacred space. Designate a quiet area at home or work where you can practice yoga, meditate, write in your journal, or daydream.

- Write a brief account of why you began (or want to begin) practicing yoga. Reread it now and again to renew your commitment to practice.

- If you find yourself wanting to study with a teacher, notice what draws you to that person. Perhaps it is his or her generosity, compassion, or patience. Consider the ways in which this quality already exists within you.

- Embrace solitude. Make a date with yourself each week to spend time alone. You could practice yoga, take a walk in nature, listen to music, or do nothing. If you choose to do nothing, do not feel guilty about it.

- Keep a list of what is important to you about living your yoga. What needs your attention? Remember, your life is a work in progress. Review the list regularly and update it to reflect your changing needs.

- Are there some aspects of yoga, such as studying the *Yoga Sutra* or developing a meditation practice, that you want to explore, but do not know how to begin? Ask a fellow student to describe how she began.

- Begin and end each day with a Mantra for Daily Living.

Mantras for Daily Living

- I am my own authority.

- My life is a work in progress.

- I desire wholeness.

- All the answers are within me.

- Life is practice: practice is life.

- I commit to living my life fully in this moment.

2

Discipline

abhyasa-vairagyabhyam tan-nirodhah
The restriction of these fluctuations is achieved
through practice and dispassion.

—*Yoga Sutra* 1:12

One of the most powerful ideas I have ever encoun-
tered was one that I read at a very difficult time in my life. My
three children were young, my husband's job was demanding,
and I was busy teaching yoga. Additionally, I spent time each
day practicing yoga and writing articles for *Yoga Journal*.
Despite my seeming success, something was wrong. I couldn't
seem to juggle my life so that I could not only get everything
done, but also get it done well. One day while browsing in a
bookstore, I picked up *The Road Less Traveled: A New
Psychology of Love, Traditional Values, and Spiritual Growth* by
Scott Peck. The very first sentence simultaneously shocked
and comforted me: "Life is difficult."[1]

Waves of relief flooded through me. Written plainly
for all to see was the truth that I had been living: my life *was*
difficult. As I pondered further, I realized something else: I
was making my life *more* difficult. This recognition was
powerful and I remember feeling a sense of physical light-
ness and mental freedom. Clearly, I had misunderstood and
misapplied the concept of discipline.

For as long as I could remember, I had spent my days
accomplishing a series of "have to's," things that I required

myself to finish before going to bed. Parents, teachers, and friends had commented positively on my ability to do so. I had incorporated their reinforcement into my self-image. In reality, my way of living my life was unsustainable. My attachment to my idea of discipline drove me to work constantly. I had confused "getting things done" with the real meaning of discipline.

Beginning with the simple wisdom of Peck, I worked with my thoughts and my behavior. I realized that although life is difficult, I did not have to approach life by becoming difficult myself. I decided to simplify my life. I began by giving up working at my desk after the children were in bed, even though it seemed as if those hours were the only quiet time I could find to write or keep up with other paperwork. Our after-dinner time became more leisurely. I actually spent some time with my husband, got more rest, and, paradoxically, began to feel that I was accomplishing more in my day.

Next, I realized that I could either pay a therapist for a once-a-week session to complain about how I was overworked, or I could pay a teenage helper to come in for a few hours four afternoons a week. I chose the latter option and ended up saving money as well as contributing to my peace of mind. It has been a road of trial and error for me, and I have learned that discipline has less to do with accomplishment and more to do with intention and with commitment.

In the *Yoga Sutra*, Patanjali discusses discipline in the first book, verse twelve: *abhyasa-vairagyabhyam tan-nirodhah,* or "The restriction of these fluctuations is achieved through practice and dispassion."[2] To elaborate on this teaching, yoga, or that state in which fluctuations (or agitations) of the mind are resolved, can be achieved by practice (or discipline) and detachment. (Detachment, or letting go, is the subject of Chapter Three.) Practice, then, is discipline in action. This is different from task-oriented behavior. Discipline is truly expressed by my intention to stay present in each moment. Whether it is driving my children to school, standing in the grocery line, paying bills, interacting with coworkers, finishing a task on time, or practicing yoga in a formal way, if I do it with a deep intimacy with each moment, then I am truly disciplined. Without that intimacy, I am merely performing a series of mechanical actions.

Several years ago, I met a woman who told me that she had begun to meditate for five minutes every morning. My initial reaction was judgmental. What a joke!, I thought. How could five minutes make any difference? In truth, she had a realistic and balanced attitude about her life and her practice. She had declared her intention, and she lived her commitment to meditate every day. She interpreted discipline as doing what was possible with consistency. I had interpreted discipline as quantity. I realized that I thought two hours of yoga practice indicated a disciplined life, whereas five minutes did not. In time, I came to realize her wisdom: Do what you can and do it fully.

Patanjali describes this as *abhyasa*, which comes from the Sanskrit roots *abhi* and *as,* and means literally "to apply oneself."[3] From this viewpoint, all of life is practice. Practice is not about what you get, it is about what you give. Whether you are driven or resistant, the medicine is the same: do what is truly possible with unwavering commitment to giving yourself to the moment. Without this intention, practice becomes another task to be completed and it loses its ability to transform. And transformation, or freedom, is the reason for all discipline.

Discipline Practice

In trying to be disciplined, you might force something unpleasant on yourself or think that you must give up something. The true spirit of abhyasa is neither. In the following exercise, you will experience how discipline and freedom are intertwined.

To begin, make a list of things that you have always wanted to do, but never seem to find the time to try, or things that you already do but have resistance to doing. You might choose meditating, writing a book, playing the piano, practicing yoga poses or breathing techniques, reading a good book, or taking a daily walk. It could be something else. What is important is that you pick something and commit yourself to doing it for fifteen minutes a day. I suggest that you do this one thing only and not combine it with another activity. Further, I recommend that you do it at the same time and in the same place each day. If this is not possible, do it where and when you can.

To support your commitment, set a timer. It is important to continue for the full fifteen minutes. It is also important to stop after fifteen minutes, so that you do not become obsessive about the activity. Some days you will want to do this exercise; other days, it may be difficult. In either case, do it anyway, acknowledging that it is something that you have chosen.

At the beginning of each day's activity, spend a few moments breathing quietly, declaring your intention to stay present throughout the activity. At the end of each day's activity, express gratitude for having taken the opportunity to practice. You might even write down the thoughts, feelings, and bodily sensations that you experienced during practice. Keep them brief. Carry on for one month, and then review your experience. At that time, you may want to continue the activity, change it, or drop it all together. In any case, you will have had the opportunity to experience consistency and commitment without rigidity. In addition, your energetic experience of this activity may be softer, smoother, more expansive, and more integrated with your other energetic experiences than when you were just thinking about doing it, forcing yourself to do it, or avoiding doing it.

Other Practice Suggestions

- Do one thing at a time.

- Commit yourself to doing what is possible. Make a list of what you have to do tomorrow; eliminate activities that are unnecessary and reschedule those that can and should be postponed.

- Take a nap every Sunday.

- Slow down. Begin each activity, such as driving, speaking at a meeting, or walking onto your commuter train, with one gentle inhalation, followed by a calm exhalation.

- Ask for help with a task.

- If you are experiencing resistance to doing yoga, begin with the Abiding Practice from Chapter One, "Spiritual Seeking," or schedule a practice date with a friend to help you get started. If your practice feels stale, take a day off.

■ Take a lunch break every day.

■ Where does the time go? No one thinks he has enough of it to take time out for himself. As I wrote in my first book, *Relax and Renew: Restful Yoga for Stressful Times,* write down what you do in one-half-hour increments, from 7:00 A.M. to 9:30 P.M., for the next three days. This exercise will help you discover free time. Rather than dragging yourself from one duty to the next, take a break. Think how restorative it would be to relax, or to practice yoga, or to paint water-colors. I guarantee that you will be more productive for having done so.

■ When you notice that you are pushing yourself to complete a task, soften and be merciful with yourself. Inhale quietly and exhale gently, extending the very same kindness to yourself that you would extend to another in the same situation. Begin again.

Mantras for Daily Living

■ I give myself fully to each moment.

■ Discipline is quality, not quantity.

■ I can always make a choice.

■ There is enough time.

■ My yoga practice is discipline in action.

3

Letting Go

abhyasa-vairagyabhyam tan-nirodhah

The restriction of these fluctuations is achieved
through practice and dispassion.

—*Yoga Sutra* 1:12

One of the most frequently studied principles of
yoga's sacred texts is the concept of letting go. Also called
detachment or surrender, letting go is an action carried out in
relationship with a religious figure or guru, with a particular
teaching, and, most important, with the nitty-gritty details of
the present moment. Letting go is difficult for most of us to
understand and to practice.

While I was discussing surrender and detachment
several years ago with a few yoga students, one of them stated
emphatically, "I tried that surrender thing once and it didn't
work." Her response gave us all a good laugh, but it was the
truth. Trying "that surrender thing once" will not do much. It
is a lifetime practice that must be built on deep understanding.

Verse twelve of book one of the *Yoga Sutra* addresses
detachment: *abhyasa-vairagyabhyam tan-nirodhah,* or "The
restriction of these fluctuations is achieved through practice
and dispassion.[1] Here Patanjali teaches that wholeness comes
from *abhyasa,* which means "to apply oneself"[2] (discussed in
Chapter Two, "Discipline"), and from *vairagya,* or "supreme
detachment."[3]

Why is detachment so difficult to understand?

17

Perhaps the problem lies in confusing being detached with being uninterested. Actually, they are opposites. If you are uninterested, you withdraw, you turn your back on life, which, in a way, denies the difficulty of life. To be detached is to stand in the middle of the marketplace, with all its confusion and noise, and to remain present to yourself and to all that is. No wonder my student was pessimistic about being able to surrender.

If we accept the importance of detachment, from what, then, do we detach? Patanjali introduces the important concept of *avidya* in the second book, verse three: *avidya-asmita-raga-dvesha-abhiniveshah panca-kleshah,* or "Nescience, I-am-ness, attachment, aversion, and the will-to-live are the five causes-of-affliction."[4] *Avidya* has three parts: *a,* the negating prefix, *vid,* "to see with the inner eye,"[5] and *ya,* the activating suffix. In literal terms, *avidya* means "actively being in the state of not seeing the true nature of reality."[6] The classical translation of *avidya* is "nescience" or "ignorance."[7] Patanjali teaches that we are caught in avidya, that is, in seeing reality from our own particular point of view.

A story can help to clarify this point. In *An American Tragedy,* novelist Theodore Dreiser writes about a young man in search of his missing father. Along the way, he visits a Native American chief and asks for his help in understanding his situation. The chief points to the woven rug covering the floor. Turning it over to reveal the myriad threads lying in a confusion of color, the chief says that this is how the world looks to us. Turning the rug right side up, the chief tells the young man to see the intricate and beautiful pattern now apparent. The chief suggests that this is the way the world looks to God.

The lesson here, of course, is that truth is a matter of perspective. So if you ask yourself from what exactly are you to be detached, the only possible answer is that you are to give up your attachment to the way you *think* things are. When you do, you get out of your own way and can experience another perspective. All the spiritual traditions talk about enlightenment or realization. One way to view enlightenment is as a radical shift in perspective. Nothing outside of you has changed: *you* have changed. And yet, paradoxically, you have *not* changed, but rather have become what you already are. You have just removed the smoke screen of ignorance so that what always had been present has become apparent.

Another aspect of surrender is that, yes, eventually we must give up everything. Some years ago, while filling out a form, I stared at the blank space in which I was to indicate my permanent address. Being in a philosophical mood, I was momentarily stumped by this question. I asked myself, What is permanent? The next question was, Do you own or rent your home? Own?, I thought. If I am honest about the answer to this question, I must admit that I own nothing. I have to give back everything when I die: my body, my feelings, my mind, my thoughts, my experiences, my education, my husband, my children, my family, my friends, my profession, and even my yoga; in short, absolutely everything that I think I am.

Patanjali's "detachment" beckons you to cultivate the willingness to surrender as you go along, right here and now, but not because you despair or are uninterested. On the contrary, detachment requires total engagement. When you allow yourself to see things as they really are, then—and only then— can you love yourself and others without hidden expectations. Detachment is the greatest act of love.

Learning the lesson of vairagya is a daily one. Recently, I took my daughter to see her orthodontist. While in the waiting room, we looked together at a book of holograms. She turned through the twenty-page book, exclaiming about the beauty of the hidden designs. I could not see even one, although she patiently explained how to do so. When she went in for her exam, I became more and more agitated and impatient because, try as I might, I still could not find the hidden images. I was angry with myself for failing. Then I felt sorry for myself for being so stupid as to have been, once again, outsmarted by technology.

In resignation, I tried one more time and, for some unknown reason, relaxed my intense focus on the pictures. At once, the hidden design jumped out at me, and I was drawn into another world, one of depth and beauty. I excitedly turned the pages, vowing not to leave until I had seen every design. Later that night, as I retold the day's events to my husband, I was struck with the power of what had happened. This was a living teaching: When I let go, I was able to see what had been there the whole time. Patanjali would have been proud.

Letting Go Practice

Learning to live with detachment is, to say the least, a challenge. I find that paying attention to those very moments when I feel attached to be an effective technique of letting go. For example, when I find myself in a surrender struggle, instead of trying to detach from whatever it is, including the struggle, I allow myself to feel my attachment completely. When I shine the spotlight of awareness on this attachment, I actually discover something else: perspective. As I become aware of my attachment, it has less power over me.

This practice can be done both on and off the yoga mat. It is difficult but rewarding beyond belief. The next time you feel yourself caught in the grip of attachment, such as wanting something to turn out a certain way, take time out—right then and there—to notice what is happening in your body. How does your belly feel? Has your breathing changed? Is your jaw tight? Your forehead drawn? Notice your bodily sensations. They are the manifestations of your attachment.

Stay present to your bodily sensations. If you try to pull surrender to you or push discomfort away, you will create even more agitation. Engage life by accepting the sensations as they are. As you continue, you may notice that you begin to relax and that your mind is not gripped so tightly around the outcome. And if this does not happen the first time you practice this exercise—or even the thirty-first time—that is okay. Just keep practicing. This, too, is surrender.

Other Practice Suggestions
- If you notice that you have a strong desire to be right, try not venturing an opinion the next time someone else expresses one.

- If you are in a situation in which you notice your attachment to the outcome of a problem, offer your help and then step back; this will free others to do the same.

- When the occasion arises, go along with what your partner or friend wants. Let her pick the restaurant or movie. Or, if you always rely on her lead, you pick. Relinquish the habit of having to be in charge or the habit of giving in.

Mantras for Daily Living

- Detachment is the greatest act of love.

- I am willing to engage life.

- This moment is the perfect moment to let go.

4

Self-Judgment

sthira-sukham asanam

The posture should be steady and comfortable.

—*Yoga Sutra* 2:46

The definition of *asana*, or "yoga pose," is found in the second book, verse forty-six, of the *Yoga Sutra: sthira-sukham asanam*, or "The posture should be steady and comfortable."[1] To some, this verse is surprising, because it does not jive with what is generally understood about this physical aspect of yoga. What could Patanjali possibly mean by "comfortable"? What about sweat, twenty-minute Headstands (*Salamba Shirshasana*), and the exercise mantra of "No pain, no gain"?

Throughout the years, I have noticed the tendency in myself and others to think that we must practice boot-camp yoga, that is, the poses must be difficult, even painful, to be beneficial and worthwhile. Sadly, we do not practice to find the comfortable, but to overcome ourselves and conquer the pose. In reality, our thoughts about the poses reflect our thoughts about ourselves. It is not uncommon for students to berate themselves with self-judging internal dialogue during practice.

I saw this tendency more clearly in myself after listening to an exchange between a friend and my daughter, who was three years old at the time. My friend asked her if she did yoga, meaning asanas. Looking up from her play, my daughter shook her head no, declaring that she did "traumayama."

(*Pranayama* is the term for "breathing exercises.") Out of the mouths of babes!, I thought. Her answer reminded me that I, too, practiced traumayama. Many times in my practice, as well as in other areas of my life, I responded from a place of judgment. Often my internal dialogue was negative and pejorative, causing me to inflict my yoga practice upon myself. And if I was doing that to myself, what was I teaching my students? How was I interacting with family and friends?

I began to pay attention to how often I judged myself. I was appalled to learn that *most* of the time my inner dialogue was self-judgmental. But what really shook me was when I discovered something even more disconcerting: there was no way that I could be harsh toward myself and, at the same time, be compassionate to others. I realized also that the process of silently putting myself down was actually a form of egoism.

If you expect more from yourself than from others, you are saying that you are better than others and, therefore, must perform at a superior level. I do not mean that you should not set goals for yourself. Rather, the question is, how do you react if you cannot meet these goals? Honestly admitting that you may have not done your best is not judgment. It *is* judgment when you draw a conclusion about yourself based on your ideas about failure. Honesty involves taking responsibility; judgment has to do with blame. To view yourself as bad or a failure because you did not accomplish what you set out to do is judgment. To state clearly and simply that you did not accomplish your plan is taking responsibility.

Another of my children taught me a great lesson about self-judgment. Recently, I was having difficulty in replacing paper in my fax machine. As my difficulty escalated, so did my inner chatter of criticism. I make it a practice to verbalize these judgments whenever possible. Hearing them makes them obvious, even ludicrous, and this helps me to let go of them.

As I continued loading the fax paper, I stated my judgments out loud: "Why am I so stupid? Why can't I do anything right?" Unbeknownst to me, my teenage son was cooking in the kitchen, and he overheard me. In the past, he had come to my aid when I needed "in-house" technological support. This day, he came into my office and said with a grin, "Mom, don't be so self-deprecating. You *can* do something right. You had me." It was a joke, but he said it with such love that I immediately started crying and hugged him. Although I may think that my critical inner dialogue is harming only me, it does affect others, in ways both direct and indirect. The power of this moment stayed with me for several days.

What Patanjali teaches about "comfortable" has relevance to the practice of yoga poses, which are not different from the practice of life itself. Learning to live in a way that is comfortable, or agreeable, to others and to the Earth is crucial. It begins when you can bring a sense of the comfortable to your inner life, to your thoughts, and to how you frame your reality by how you speak to yourself.

The translation of the first word in Patanjali's verse is interesting. The word *sthira* means "steady."[2] Although not the same Sanskrit word as discussed in Chapter One, "Spiritual Seeking," for me, *sthira* also has a feeling of "abiding."[3] *To abide* is "to remain present with a sense of fullness."[4] When you resort to self-judgment, you are no longer present, you are no longer practicing. Learning to be present with yourself and to abide in that which is "steady and comfortable" does not allow space for self-judgment. When you live this way, you are practicing yoga: you are living fully.

Finally, another family incident taught me about the power of self-judgment. When our three children were small, their tradition was to create a whole bag full of brightly colored and glittering homemade Father's Day cards. They would "surprise" their dad while he was still in bed, ceremoniously handing him the cards, one by one, until several dozen had been given out. One year, after the oldest had learned to write but not to spell, they presented him with a big card that said, "Happy Father's Day, Dad. We love you. Just be your *slef*." Of course, they could not have known how endearing this misspelling was, and how important it was to us that they understand this life message. Since that day, I have reflected on being my *slef* many times as I have wrestled with my lack of self-acceptance and my continued self-judgment.

My *Slef* Practice

If you are to free yourself of thoughts of self-judgment, then first you must be aware of them. Try this exercise. Taking your physical limitations and health into account, pick a yoga pose that is difficult, if not impossible, for you to do. Practice, or rather attempt to practice, this pose every day for one month.

To begin, say silently or out loud, "I am attempting something difficult, and I appreciate myself for trying." Then pay close attention to your internal dialogue as you practice the pose. At times, you may even talk yourself through the pose out loud. Listen to the instructions you give yourself about the physical aspects of how to do the pose. Whose instructions are they? Your own? A teacher's? What do you say to yourself when you succeed? When you fail? When you are somewhere in between? Can you do the pose just to do the pose? Can your dialogue become agreeable? Is the pose quiet and steady? When you come out of the pose, say aloud, "I have tried something difficult, and I appreciate myself for trying."

When you feel comfortable in the pose, pick another one and repeat the process. Then try something that is difficult in another area of your life. Remember, the difficulty might never change, but your attitude and inner dialogue can.

Other Practice Suggestions

- You can write down your internal dialogue right after the My *Slef* Practice. Keep your jottings brief. Do not try to interpret them. It will be interesting to note if or how the dialogue changes throughout time.

- If you find yourself forcing in asana (or in any other part of your life), ask yourself, Is this in the spirit of yoga or is this traumayama?

- If you notice that someone else is judging you, don't be quick to agree or to internalize the judgment. Think about what happened and agree only if his assessment aligns with yours.

- If you are going into a situation about which you feel anxious, tense, or afraid, say to yourself, I am perfect just as I am.

■ Rather than approaching your yoga practice from an attitude of no pain, no gain, how about no pain, no pain?

■ Do not criticize yourself, anyone else, or anything for one hour. If this feels like too much, commit to doing this for the next five minutes.

Mantras for Daily Living

■ I commit to just being my *slef*.

■ No pain, no pain.

■ Perfection is an illusion.

■ I am attempting something difficult,
  and I appreciate myself for trying.

■ I am perfect just as I am.

■ Am I practicing yoga or traumayama?

■ I am choosing to let go of my self-judgment now.

⌒

5

Faith

shraddha-virya-smriti-samadhi-prajna-purvaka itaresham
Wholeness is preceded by faith, energy, mindfulness, union,
and awareness.

—*Yoga Sutra* 1:20

As children, my brother and I waited on Christmas
Eve with agonizing intensity for the arrival of Santa Claus.
We had total belief not only in Santa's existence, but also
that he would leave packages under our tree, even though
we did not have a chimney. Unlike some kids who learned
suddenly that there is no Santa Claus, we were lucky
enough to gradually realize on our own that he is not a real
person, but represents the spirit of giving that is Christmas.

Years later, when I had my own children, I began to
think more philosophically about the power of belief, not only
in relationship to Santa Claus, but also to the rest of my life.
I noticed that when I used the word *belief,* my perception was
controlled by a set of predetermined ideas about the situation
or the person at hand. I came to see my beliefs as filters
through which I interpreted everything around me. I began
to pay attention to the times I used "belief." It seemed that
when I did, I was thinking or talking about something that
could not change. For example, I had certain beliefs about
my physical abilities, especially in relationship to yoga poses.
When I began practicing yoga, I would look at some of the
more exotic poses with the belief that I could never do them.

After many years of diligent practice, I find that I can do them and have been able to side-step my so-called beliefs.

As I studied the *Yoga Sutra,* I noticed that Patanjali used the word *faith* rather than *belief.* Why? I decided to read one sutra at a time from different translations and let the meaning sink in throughout days or weeks. From this practice, I came to understand that belief is a preconception about the way reality should be; faith is the willingness to experience reality as it is, including the acceptance of the unknown. An interesting way to understand the difference is to use the words interchangeably in the same sentence: I believe in Santa Claus. I have faith in Santa Claus. Belief can impede spiritual unfoldment; faith is supremely necessary for it.

In verse twenty, book one, of the *Yoga Sutra,* Patanjali states the importance of faith to spiritual practice: *shraddha-virya-smriti samadhi-prajna-purvaka itaresham,* or "Wholeness is preceded by faith, energy, mindfulness, union, and awareness."[1] The practices of yoga, which include poses, breathing, meditation, and self-awareness techniques, are difficult in and of themselves. It is also difficult to practice consistently in the midst of our busy lives. In order to commit ourselves to practice, we must have faith that they will be fruitful and accomplish their intent, which is to help us turn toward ourselves and recognize our essential wholeness.

Faith is a recipe made up of part trust in ourselves, part experience of life working out, and part intuitive connection with the Divine. There is a knowingness about faith that instills assurance in the faithful. One day, while walking in the woods, my then three-year-old daughter asked me who had made the trees. I responded that God had made them when he had made the world. She whirled around, hands on her hips, cocked her head to one side, and said in that supremely confident way so common to the very young, "Mommy, don't you know that God's a she, too?" Faced with such pure faith, I could do nothing but respond, "Of course."

Faith has an innocence and a certainty that I find an alluring quality in others and comforting one in myself. Faith is the quiet cousin of Courage. Faith is willing to put its foot out when there is no guarantee that there will be a step to support it. Without faith, we cannot make the most important decisions of life: when and if to become a parent, whether to move across the country to take a new job, when a relationship should be ended, and myriad others.

But in what are we to have faith? Basically, we are to have faith in just about everything. The mystery of the Universe and our existence in it demands faith in everything from the mundane to the spectacular: from the workers who built our house so that it will stay up over our heads during the night while we sleep to the cycling of the seasons. There is a comforting Japanese folk Zen saying that poignantly reminds us of the necessity of faith:

> Everything
>
> Changes in this world
>
> > But flowers will open
>
> Each spring
>
> Just as usual.[2]

For those practicing yoga, Patanjali states that we must first have faith in the efficacy of the practices of yoga. Unless we have faith in the ability of these practices to facilitate self-transformation, we will be unable to continue them when the going gets difficult, boring, or demanding. Next, he suggests that we have faith in the teachers, both living and dead, who can share their experience with us through their living teachings and, more significantly, through their examples. Finally, faith in ourselves is the *most* important prerequisite to the study of yoga. Having faith in yourself honors that inner knowing that guides you unerringly home to the Divine.

Faith Practice

A dear friend and teacher of yoga died recently. At her memorial service, it was said that during her life she "made the hard decisions with a soft heart." To me, this is the essence of faith. When we have faith in ourselves and others, we are able to make difficult decisions when necessary. But at the same time, we do not lose the compassion and softness inside that connects us to others. When I lose faith in myself or in the Universe, my decisions are more likely to be made out of fear or anger. If I try to make life's difficult decisions without connecting with my heart, I do not act in the best interests of all concerned. My faith is most apparent when I have the courage to act from my heart and the compassion to stay open. This is the ultimate expression of faith. I am reminded of another Japanese folk Zen saying:

> Fish live in streams
> Birds nest in trees
> Human beings dwell
> In warm hearts.[3]

To keep the faith, recite both Japanese folk Zen sayings in this chapter. They will help to soothe you during trying times and strengthen your resolve in lighter moments.

Other Practice Suggestions

- Using complete sentences, write down the things in which you believe. Rewrite the list, replacing *believe* with *faith*.

- Do you have a favorite nature spot in your garden or in the park near where you work? Visit it as often as you can. Notice how the plants, trees, and even the sky overhead changes with the seasons. Depending on where you live, the changes may be subtle. Nevertheless, all is as it should be.

Mantras for Daily Living

- I have faith in myself.

- I have the courage to act from my heart and the compassion to stay open.

- I have faith in yoga.

- I am willing to make the hard decisions with a soft heart.

- I have faith in my willingness to have faith.

- Faith is the quiet cousin of Courage.

6

Perspective

viveka-khyatir-aviplava hana-upayah

The means of attaining cessation is the unceasing vision
of discernment.

—*Yoga Sutra* 2:26

In Chapter Three, "Letting Go," I described how my
trying to see the holograms in a book actually prevented my
discovering them. Although necessary in yoga practice and in
facing life's challenges, effort can actually also be an obstacle.
In book two, verse twenty-six, of the *Yoga Sutra,* Patanjali
writes, *viveka-khyatir-aviplava hana-upayah,* or "The means of
attaining cessation is the unceasing vision of discernment."[1]
His teaching implies two important things about effort. First,
whatever we need to see is right in front of us. How often do
we forget to look homeward for answers to the questions of
life? As I discussed in Chapter One, "Spiritual Seeking," many
of the great teachers have told us that the answers can be
found within us. Sadly, we often forget to trust the whisperings
of our own hearts.

Second, Patanjali teaches that the power of discrimination helps us to better understand the nature of reality.
Another way to describe this is to say that we can benefit from
maintaining perspective about what is happening in life—right
here, right now. Even though I finally could see the holograms,
nothing about the holograms had changed. The holograms were
there and I was there. However, I benefited from shifting my

perspective, first by relaxing and then by changing my visual focus. When we cling to one point of view, we limit our ability to see what is before us. Enlightenment, in fact, is nothing more and nothing less than a radical change of perspective.

Life will continually challenge us. If we pay attention, these challenges can broaden our perspective. One day, I walked into my son's room and asked him to pick up the things that cluttered the floor. I told him that he needed to create some order out of his chaos. Turning to look at me, he said dryly, "But, Mom, don't you know that order is just chaos repeated twice." Speechless, I quietly left the room. I certainly learned an interesting lesson that day in the power of perspective!

So much of what we call wisdom is really the clarity of perspective. When we step back and allow perspective to be part of our process of perception, we are using the discrimination of which Patanjali speaks. With our willingness to have perspective, not only do we increase our ability to distinguish the important from the unimportant, we also increase our capacity for compassion toward ourselves and others. By paying attention to how we lose perspective about little things, as I did in my escapade with the holograms, we can create a habit of opening our perspective to accommodate the more important things. We will be more likely to understand what is actually permanent and lasting and what is not.

A story illustrates the point. One day, a monk was walking by the banks of a lake and found an abandoned rowboat. He spent several months lovingly restoring it. Finally, the day came to launch it on the clear waters of the lake. As he began to row, he noticed that it was getting foggy, but he continued nonetheless. Suddenly, swiftly cutting through the fog came another rowboat, which rammed into his boat. All of his work—the new wood and the paint job—was damaged. The monk got angry and strained to see who had done this thoughtless thing to his beautiful boat. And then he saw that the other boat was empty. His anger collapsed in the moment.

So much of our suffering is linked to effort and to reactions that are tied to an iron-clad perspective. When the monk took a good look at what had happened, he moved from reaction to having perspective. Perhaps Patanjali is trying to teach us that at least some of the annoying events and people in our lives are simply empty rowboats.

Perspective Practice

Let me tell you another story. A villager lived in a small house with his wife, mother-in-law, six children, a cow, and some chickens. It was driving him crazy. So he went to the village rabbi and asked for help. The rabbi said that he could solve the problem: he advised the man to buy a goat. Overjoyed, the man immediately went out and bought a goat. Now he had a wife, a mother-in-law, six children, a cow, some chickens, and a goat. The house was even more chaotic than before. The villager returned to the rabbi and described the increased chaos. Once again the rabbi said that he could solve the problem. He told the man to sell the goat. Obediently, the villager went home and sold his goat. Suddenly, all he had in his small house were his wife, his mother-in-law, his six kids, a cow, and some chickens. Things were positively peaceful without that goat.

Borrowing from this story, I decided to make a Mantra for Daily Living this chapter's main practice. When you find yourself in a situation that could be made better if you were to step back to gain perspective, inhale gently and on your next exhalation, say to yourself, Sell the goat. Consider posting the mantra in places where it would be helpful to be reminded to soften your grip on your point of view: in your datebook, in your yoga practice space, inside a file folder that you must take into a meeting, near the telephone, or on the edge of your computer screen. Your life is as it is. How you feel about your life is up you.

Other Practice Suggestions

- Make a two-column list. In one, list some things or people that you experience as difficult. In the other, write down simple ways to help you gain perspective. For example, you have an upcoming social event that you dread. In column one, write down all the reasons that you antici- pate the difficulty, such as the reason for the gathering, some of the people who will be there, or something else. In column two, note what is important to you about the event and at least one thing that you like about each attendee. Although this exercise cannot guarantee smooth sailing, it can help you soften your dread and widen your perspective.

- As you practice yoga, notice your intention and your degree of effort. Are they helpful? Do you need to step back and reevaluate?

- Make a trade agreement with a friend. Wash his dishes and let him wash yours. Someone else's dishes are always more interesting.

- Lie on the bed with your child and "hang out." Just be there as she does her homework or reads a book. Imagine the stresses of being a kid today. Tell her that you appreciate the difficulties of her life.

- Cultivate gratitude. Write a list of all the things about your life or about someone you love for which you are grateful.

Mantras for Daily Living
- The rowboat is empty.

- Soften and be merciful.

- Sell the goat.

- It won't be this way forever.

- The worse could happen; the best could happen. Life is usually somewhere in between.

7

Courage

avinashi tu tad viddhi
  yena sarvam idam tatam
vinasham avyayasyasya
  na kashcit kartum arhati

Yet, know as indestructable that by which this whole world is
spread out. No one is able to accomplish the destruction of that
which is immutable.

—*Bhagavad Gita* 2:17

I find it interesting that we believe that both love and
courage reside within the heart. I am reminded of the coward-
ly lion in *The Wizard of Oz* who discovered that the path to
courage was through the heart, and of how we tell people who
are afraid to "take heart." I think that, after the ability to love
one's self and others, courage is the second most important
quality to cultivate in life. I have been taught repeatedly the
importance of true courage, which I have come to see as equal
parts knowing what is possible for me and understanding my
interdependence with the world around me.

Each summer, I visit the Tassajara Zen Mountain
Center, in Carmel Valley, California, where I teach the yoga
portion of a workshop that integrates the disciplines of Zen and
yoga. My family likes to accompany me, and my children spend
their days in nature. One year, when they were still fairly young,
they hiked to the rapids, an old-fashioned swimming hole
where there were large boulders from which to jump into dark,
cool waters, far from the dry heat of the Tassajara summer.

My daughter was five and very determined never to be left out when her two older brothers plunged ahead in life. After the boys jumped off the largest rock, she climbed up and jumped, too. When asked where she got the courage when even adults found it daunting to jump off that rock, she replied, "I have a girl's courage." "What is that?," I asked. "Brave, but not foolish," came her reply. I intend no disparagement to boys or men by telling this story. However, I guess that she had seen her brothers do other things that she considered foolish. She saw the difference between doing something foolish just to appear brave and doing something that actually required courage. This is, of course, a crucial distinction.

In yoga classes, there are times when you are challenged by the teacher to try something that, either for physical or for emotional reasons, is frightening. The challenge may be what the teacher thinks you need, and to meet it, you must call upon your courage. But how do you choose action? How do you differentiate between taking care of yourself and your need to overcome resistance or fear? One way is to take an inventory of where you are in the moment: What is possible for me? What is in my heart? Do I want to do this? Is it appropriate for me? Do I trust this teacher in this situation? Do I need more help than what is being offered? Do I understand that I am not alone and can ask for help? Whatever you decide, know that courage is not forcing yourself to do something because you want to be accepted, or don't want to look like a coward or be embarrassed. You express foolishness when you simply acquiesce, unwilling or unable to find your voice to object or decline.

You can strengthen your courage muscle by acknowledging to yourself how many times a day you choose to act from true courage.

In book two, verse seventeen, the *Bhagavad Gita* states, *avinashi tu tad viddhi / yena sarvam idam tatam / vinasham avyayasyasya / na kashcit kartum arhati,* or "Yet, know as indestructable that by which this whole world is spread out. No one is able to accomplish the destruction of that which is immutable."[1] Lord Krishna tells the hero Arjuna, metaphorically speaking, that there is no reason for him to cower under the bed, hiding from life and duty. He assures Arjuna that all is pervaded by Spirit and there is nothing to fear. Krishna wants Arjuna to forge ahead, trusting in his oneness with God. The *Bhagavad Gita* describes this connection as "immutable."

I resonate with this teaching because those times when I have been the most afraid were when I felt disconnected from God, from Spirit, from the Universe, from family and friends, and, most important, from my own heart. Courage cannot exist in isolation. Just as a flower needs sun, air, soil, and water to bloom, your courage depends on your interdependence with people and things. You must contemplate deeply to understand that when you do what is possible, you are not in a free fall, but are cradled by your interdependence with the world around you. For example, you may decide to marry or to have a child, quit a job, risk an investment, explore your emotional past, or sign up to go back to college after many years' absence. Your work is to distinguish what is important enough to require your commitment and what is not worthy of your courage. You can rest assured that when you act from true courage, the people, the tools, and your own inner knowing needed for the heroine's journey will be available to you.

Courage Practice

Many times I think that I lack courage because I feel that I must accomplish a difficult task without feeling afraid. The most important thing to know about courage is that it cradles your action *even though* you are afraid. To understand your relationship with courage, pick a yoga pose that you find somewhat frightening, but one that you are physically able to do. For many, this may be an inversion, such as Handstand (*Adho Mukha Vrkshasana*) done at the wall.

Practice this pose every day, but begin slowly. How long you hold the pose is not important. On the first day, simply find a place in your house where you can practice. On day two, go to your practice area and work with the beginning of the basic variation of Handstand. Sit on the floor with your feet touching the baseboard. Put your hands by the sides of your hips. This is where your hands will be when you practice the variation. Next, turn around and position your hands at that place on the floor and kneel down. Lift your knees slightly and then lift *only* one foot and place it on the wall. Allow your hands to bear some of your body weight.

The next day, repeat day two, and add a little more weight. Repeat this for as many days as you need to until you are able to lift first one leg, and then the other. In the final position of this variation, your body should be in the shape of an L, with your feet on the wall and your hands on the floor.

As you work with the pose, notice when fear arises and when your courage helps you. Notice, too, when you feel ready to reach out for help from a qualified yoga teacher to work on full Handstand at the wall.

Keep up the rhythm of your practice. Remember, the point is not to do something just because it is scary. The point is to choose to do what is possible in the face of fear. That choice defines courage. And with it comes a sense of freedom.

Other Practice Suggestions

- Pick one person and, when appropriate, tell her something that you have long wanted or needed to say to her. Do this with love and compassion. Listen to her response in the same spirit.

- Remind yourself about how much courage it takes just to live in today's world. Spend a quiet moment in active appreciation of your courage.

- Refuse to tell a lie, even a small one, today. Don't agree when you don't. Remember to speak from love and to listen with compassion.

Mantras for Daily Living

- I will do what is possible.

- My courage is an expression of my love.

- Courage is the willingness to act in the face of the unknown.

- Living fully in each moment is a radical form of courage.

- Letting go of what I cannot change celebrates my courage.

PART TWO

Widening the Circle: Yoga and Relationships

8

Compassion

maitri-karuna-mudita-upekshanam sukha-duhkha-punya-
apunya-vishayanam bhavanatash-citta-prasadanam

The projection of friendliness, compassion, gladness, and
equanimity towards objects—be they joyful, sorrowful, meritorious,
or demeritorious—bring about the pacification of consciousness.

—*Yoga Sutra* 1:33

Although traditionally a solitary practice, yoga offers
great potential for transformation during those times when
we are off the mat. For me, the strength of my yoga is not
necessarily tested during my practice of poses or breathing
techniques, but in my intimate relationships. Here my anger,
attachments, and fears are not so easily hidden under a man-
tle of denial, avoidance, or achievement. In this section of
Living Your Yoga, I explore the circumstances of interaction
that can be studied in the laboratory of these relationships.

Patanjali does not discuss relationships very often in
the *Yoga Sutra*. In book two, verse thirty, he indirectly mentions
them when he talks about the *yama,* or "restraints": *ahimsa-*
satya-asteya-brahmacarya-aparigraha yamah, or "Non-harming,
truthfulness, non-stealing, chastity, and greedlessness are the
restraints."[1] In addition, Patanjali advises us to choose the high
ground in our relationships in a second reference found in book
one, verse thirty-three: *maitri-karuna-mudita-upekshanam*
sukha-duhkha-punya-apunya-vishayanam bhavanatash-citta-
prasadanam, or "The projection of friendliness, compassion,
gladness, and equanimity towards objects—be they joyful,

sorrowful, meritorious, or demeritorious—bring about the pacification of consciousness."[2]

I have chosen to focus on compassion. Traditions other than yoga also underscore the importance of compassion. Jesus tells us, "Love one another" (1 John 3:23). Although the Dalai Lama describes himself as "a simple monk," he is regarded as a reincarnation of Avalokiteshvara, the Buddha of Compassion. In Japan, this Buddha is called Kannon, or "she who hears the cries of the world."

What is compassion? For whom are we to feel it? When? How do we learn to hear the cries of the world? The word is derived from the Latin prefix *com-* and the Latin word *pati* and means literally "to suffer with."[3] In book one, verse thirty-three of the *Yoga Sutra,* Patanjali implies that compassion is to be expressed to everyone, all the time. He promises that to do so will purify us. But just as with the amity, dispassion, and goodwill that Patanjali encourages, expressing compassion is definitely a learn-as-you-go process. It is also cumulative. We can strengthen our ability to be compassionate by repeatedly expressing compassion.

But compassion does not develop in isolation from the rest of our lives. Consider the apple you bought for lunch. Your eating it is the result of many conditions, such as seeds, sun, water, wind, soil, trees, farmers, truckers, store clerks, as well as the efforts of many other unseen people and things. Compassion, too, is interdependent with many conditions. It necessarily begins with your willingness to be compassionate. It is always a partner of wisdom, which is gained from experience. And this experience leads directly back to compassion.

The old axiom wins out: Charity begins at home. So, too, with compassion. You must begin with yourself. To be compassionate toward others, you must first understand that you suffer. This awareness allows you to see that others suffer, too, and to respond with clarity to this condition, which is shared by all living beings. One of the world's most well known spiritual teachers came from India. He was called Buddha, or "awakened one." In his first teaching after his enlightenment, he imparted the Four Noble Truths. The basis of all Buddhist teaching, they go straight to the heart of the matter of being alive: the truth of suffering; the truth of the origin of suffering; the truth of the end of suffering; and the truth of the path that leads to the end of suffering.

I remember the first class I took on Buddhism. When the teacher introduced Buddha's first Noble Truth, I found the discussion slightly irritating. I began to wriggle in my seat. Why did he say that all of existence is marked by suffering? I was not suffering. I had plenty to eat, a warm home, a loving husband, and work I enjoyed. As the discussion progressed, I became increasingly agitated, finally arguing with the teacher that there was no way that this could be true for me, and that it was obvious to me that I was definitely not suffering. The irony of the situation was lost on me until sometime later. It finally dawned on me that I had just proven the truth of the teaching through my immediate defensiveness, anger, and lack of self-awareness. Inside, I was suffering deeply. I suffered primarily because of my desire for a life that was "perfect" and to keep it that way. When honest about my emotional life, I saw that my upheavals were generally related to this desire. As I began to understand the difficulties that had existed in my family of origin and the challenges of my marriage, I came to see how these situations were reflected in my clinging to the idea of a perfect life. And with this realization, I gained some wisdom and some compassion toward myself.

As a parent, I have often wrestled with what it means to be compassionate toward my children. When do I back off and let them learn life's lessons, and when do I step in and protect them from a lesson that is too brutal given their emotional maturity? Like most important questions, this one does not have a pat answer. I have learned that the most compassionate response I can have is to be willing not to judge their behavior, but to try to see the situation from their points of view. This does not mean that I forfeit my opinion on the most effective course of action they might choose. Rather, I have the intention to truly feel the situation from their narrow views, thus stepping back from my own narrow view.

Teaching compassion is both important and difficult. This became clear to me one day at a neighborhood park. As I watched my son dig in the sandbox, another child tried to take his shovel. I watched as the boy's mother explained why he couldn't have it. I watched as my son moved away from the shovel and as the other child seized the coveted object. Finally, I watched as my son came back for the shovel and the fight began. If you are concerned that I withdrew my parenting, I did not. When the fight started, I definitely was part of the process, talking to my son about sharing with others. I felt compassion for all of us—my son, the other child, his mother, and myself—in our oh-so-human reactions. Although I guided my son to make the choice to share, I still felt compassion for his reluctance to do so. With lots of encouragement, he finally did let the other boy use the shovel, and they actually began to play together. I had tried to guide my two-year-old toward the things we often forget: sharing and trust. As adults, we continue to fight over the shovel in the sandbox, only now it is a country, or oil, or religion.

On another day, I had yet another opportunity. I had purchased a new ball for my children, and we headed for the park. After several hours of play, they had had their fill of the ball. A young boy asked us if he and his friends could play with it. Trusting him, I agreed. He went off and we never saw him or the ball again. While driving home, I realized that this was a perfect opportunity to teach compassion. I asked my kids how they felt. One by one, they told me. I asked each to remember that exact feeling if they ever thought of stealing something from someone else, and to let those feelings shape their choice. Instead of being upset about the eight dollars wasted from a young family's tight budget, I was actually grateful to that boy for the lesson that he had provided.

I think a lot about compassion when I teach yoga. I tell students who are studying to be teachers, "Don't be a yoga teacher unless you are willing to create pain." In other words, I ask people to try challenging things. Even in the most gentle of classes, I call upon my students to be willing to move into physical, emotional, and mental spaces that may be uncomfortable. Yet my intention is love. I learned a long time ago that growth is sometimes painful. I summarize it for my students this way: "Good things are sometimes difficult, but not all difficult things are good." If I respect my students, I must be willing to ask them to experience the painful as well as the pleasurable, so that they can become richer, more whole, and more loving human beings. There is, of course, a vast difference between encouraging my student to grow at her own rate and simply using the power of my personality or my authority in the classroom to coerce her into doing something that she does not want to do. The student and I must both practice compassion—toward ourselves and toward each other. When we act from the heart of compassion, we always know what to do.

Compassion Practice

To increase your ability to extend compassion to others, begin by allowing compassion for yourself to grow. At a workshop on leadership that I recently attended, a fellow participant said, "Plant a potato, get a potato." Borrowing from his sage advice, I say, "Plant compassion, get compassion."

Find a quiet time and place to relax and lie comfortably on the floor in Basic Relaxation Pose (*Shavasana*). Place a small pillow or other support under your head and a larger one under your knees. Close your eyes and relax. Spend a few moments breathing slowly and easily. When you are ready, recall a past experience in which you wish that you had acted differently or in which your actions were not freely chosen.

As you recall your experience, first pay attention to your bodily sensations. What do you notice? Perhaps you feel a tightness in your throat, or a heaviness in your belly, or a restriction in your breathing. Whatever you feel, be present, with kindness.

Next, imagining that your experience is on a video-cassette, rewind and rerun it from the beginning. This time, see yourself through the perspective of time and compassion. Acknowledge that the choices you made were the best that you could do at that time. Allow your actions to be understood from your new perspective. Then slowly begin to bring your concentration to the here and now. Breathe quietly for a few minutes. Slowly roll over onto your side, open your eyes, and use your arms to help you get up.

Use this exercise at least once a week to reestablish your connection with your own compassionate nature. As this connection is strengthened, your compassion for others will grow. And, as Patanjali promises, you will be purified.

Other Practice Suggestions

- The next time someone asks you for help that is possible for you to give, lend a hand—just because you were asked.

- Speak about compassion with someone whom you experience as compassionate. Use that person as your model for developing compassion.

- Designate one day a month as Compassion Day. If you are like many of us, you have a strict internal judge and jury, and could easily list off the instances when you were not compassionate. Instead, strengthen your compassion muscle by focusing on the positive. Write down all the ways in which you were compassionate. Pick at least one way, and repeat it the next day.

- Before you go into your next meeting, to your next family

party, or to your next dinner with friends, declare your intention to yourself, I have compassion for myself and for others. See what happens.

■ If you are able, do some volunteer work within your community.

■ Remember that the compassion you have for yourself is the greatest gift you can give to others. Notice how often during the day you judge yourself. When a judgmental thought arises, consciously replace it with a compassionate thought. Some suggestions are, I am deserving of compassion today, or I am doing the best I can right now.

Mantras for Daily Living

■ I have compassion for myself.
I have compassion for others.

■ When I act from the heart of compassion,
I always know what to do.

■ Plant compassion, get compassion.

■ Compassion comes from clarity
and creates clarity.

☞

9

Control

tat-param purusha-khyater-guna-vaitrishnyam

The superior form of this dispassion is the non-thirsting
for the primary-constituents of Nature which results
from the vision of the Self.

—*Yoga Sutra* 1:16

"Life only demands the strength you possess. Only one feat is possible—not to have run away," writes Dag Hammarskjöld.[1] Sadly, we sometimes turn away from our strengths in a number of direct and indirect ways, including those times when we try to control all that is within our purview. Although it may seem that our attempt to control engages us with life, in fact it blocks us from connecting with others—or with ourselves.

In book one, verse sixteen, of the *Yoga Sutra,* Patanjali advises, *tat-param purusha-khyater-guna-vaitrishnyam,* or "The superior form of this dispassion is the non-thirsting for the primary-constituents of Nature which results from the vision of the Self."[2] In short, he counsels us to give up our attachment to controlling what we see around us. I realize that any discussion of control smacks of some New Age double-speak. Regardless, a paradox prevails: The more we try to control our world, the less control we have. The more we are willing to let go of control and simply stay present with what is, the more control we have.

Some interesting facts underscore how illusory it is to think that we are in control of very much. For example, the sun and planets are moving at 41,000 m.p.h. in an outer spiral arm of our galaxy, the Milky Way. This galaxy contains one hundred billion stars and measures one hundred thousand light years from side to side. The Earth goes around the center of the galaxy every two hundred million years. Finally, our galaxy is only one of millions of billions of galaxies. The only reasonable response to such humbling information is to realize that all of this happened and continues to happen not because of us but in spite of us.

Control is our attempt to keep at arm's length our feelings of being out of control. It springs from the fear that unhappiness and death will overwhelm us. It is certain that both will find us at some time, in some place. What we get from trying to control everything—by behaving in a demanding or manipulative manner—are lives that are even more difficult. Trying to control things is seldom a satisfying experience and does not give us what we truly want: our lives in balance.

Suzuki Roshi, founder of the San Francisco Zen Center and author of *Zen Mind, Beginner's Mind: Informal Talks on Zen Meditation and Practice,* is quoted in Les Kaye's *Zen at Work: A Zen Teacher's 30-Year Journey in Corporate America,* with the following response to a question about teenagers: "Their behavior is beyond your control."[3] His words stopped me in my tracks. As a mother of three teenagers, I realized that I could no longer physically make my almost-grown-up children do what I wanted. If I wanted to influence their behavior, it had to be through my own. The only real control I had was the choice of my own words and actions, including being clear about my expectations and needs. For example, if my thirteen-year-old wanted to go somewhere that I felt was inappropriate, such as to a rock concert until 2:00 A.M., I could really control only my response to the request. Some possibilities include the following: I could refuse to drive, refuse to pay for the ticket, and state the consequences of what would happen if he went without my approval. But there was really no way that I could prevent him from going unless I was ready to chain him to his bed or stand by with an armed guard. These alternatives must sound ludicrous, but they drive home the point: we cannot control the behavior of others. And, more important, any attempt to do so will backfire.

International peacemaker Marshall B. Rosenberg, author of *Nonviolent Communication: A Language of Compassion,* and founder and director of The Center for Nonviolent Communication, makes this point in a slightly different way. In a workshop I attended, he explained that what he had learned from his children was that he couldn't make them do anything.[4] And if by some miracle he did, they would make him wish that he hadn't. Dr. Rosenberg explained that if you coerce your child into doing something, you will pay a price. For example, even if you could exert enough control to make him take out the garbage, he would make you pay for getting your way. How often have we exerted some form of what we thought was control over our children only to have them pay us back by withdrawing, being angry, or forgetting something important to us? If we try to control the behavior of others, we may get what we want but we won't enjoy it. If we have the thought that we are making someone do what we want without eliciting their true cooperation, that control is the greatest of illusions.

I have observed my yoga students attempting to control their bodies by forcing themselves into yoga poses. I have certainly done this myself on more than one occasion— and even attained the pose by this method. But the pose was never particularly sweet or satisfying. It took me many years to realize that the practice of yoga has to do with letting go of control much more than gaining it. A perfect example is what happens in a forward bending pose. When practicing, it is difficult, if not impossible, to force a forward bending pose. And when forced, injury almost certainly results. The pose is truly accomplished only when the hamstring muscles, located in the backs of the thighs, let go, so that the pelvis can tip forward and the torso can move toward the legs. Pulling yourself forward only creates the opposite result. To bend forward safely, wait for the muscles to respond and to accommodate to what is being asked of them.

When I first became a vegetarian, it was much less popular than it is today. I subscribed to a health magazine to learn more about this new way of eating. After a year or so, I realized that the magazine was really advocating that I control my health rather than enjoy it. The editorial thrust of the articles seemed to be that I could be happy if I just determined the right combination of vitamins and minerals for my body. The unspoken promise was that I would have a perfect life.

As you will recall from Chapter Eight, "Compassion," I certainly did not need to reinforce this thought! So I stopped reading the magazine so assiduously and began to trust that my body would lead me toward health.

But where does letting go of control end and taking responsibility for my life begin? We must understand (and accept) what it is exactly that we can control and what we cannot control. In the final analysis, we can control only ourselves. But we are often dismayed at our inability to master even this. What prevents us? When we feel out of control, it is usually when there is a conflict between what we think and what we feel. Our feelings may scream one thing while our minds demand something else. But our bodies, which are the storage units for our feelings, simply cannot lie. Whatever we feel in our bodies is our truth. For example, the resistance that we feel in a yoga pose is not the problem. It may be exactly what we need, and certainly gives us the opportunity to let go of control. Working within the limits of the resistance means that we let go into exactly how the body is in this moment. We must be willing to do the pose as it is today, not how we think it should be. We may not like it, but it is the bedrock truth for us in that moment. Refusing to acknowledge this will create conflict.

Think about someone you know whom you consider to be a "control freak." I think that it is safe to say that this describes someone who desperately wants to control others and the world around her because she feels completely out of control. This type of person may appear to be tightly wound and have a rigid quality to her body and movements. Her sense of being out of control comes from unacknowledged and powerful feelings sent from the body to knock on the door of her consciousness. The great paradox about control is that when we acknowledge and actually let ourselves feel those pushed-down feelings, change begins to happen.

Let me describe this process of change. When we acknowledge and befriend powerful feelings, these previously hidden demons have less power over us. What results is space for inner quiet. From the quietness, we can make healthier choices about our actions. From choice comes freedom. From freedom comes wholeness. And wholeness is state of yoga that I spoke of in Chapter One, "Spiritual Seeking."

The real hope that we have of positively affecting our lives and our relationships is the process of working with the blocks that prevent us from being in the flow of this very moment. When we do, a magical thing happens. We live in the center of the greatest strength of all: the love that holds the Universe together and that fills our hearts.

Control Practice

Try this practice regularly with someone who is close to you. During a twenty-four-hour period, allow the other person to take the lead. If he wants the radio on in the car, do not object. If he wants the radio off, do not object. Let him determine the temperature, what movie you go to, or what you have for dinner.

I am not suggesting that you give up your good sense or preferences, but rather that you give up your attempt to control all the details of your life, particularly the things that do not really matter. I have tried this practice, and it has been both irritating and enlightening. Learning to give up the attempt to control all the small aspects of life will point out clearly how much you hold on to the need to be in charge. Good luck.

Other Practice Suggestions

■ Try this experiment. Find a quiet time and place. In Seated Mountain Pose (*Tadasana,* variation) or in Basic Relaxation Pose (*Shavasana*), sit or lie comfortably, with the spine long and the chest open. Close your eyes and bring your attention to your breath. Focus on the easy and natural flow of inhalation and exhalation and the pauses in between the two. You'll probably find that as soon as you begin to pay attention to your breath, you will begin to change it. This is the ego in action. Do not pull the breath toward you or push the ego away. Rest somewhere in between, just following the movements of the breath. Practice this exercise whenever you think that you need to control everything and everyone around you. It is a reminder, one that is both eye-opening and humbling.

■ Admit to yourself when you have made a mistake. If you can, admit it to the other person whom you have wronged through this mistake.

■ Do you always stand in the same place in your regular yoga class? Without compromising your ability to see and hear the teacher and learn from your fellow students, pick a different spot. Notice if this gives you a new perspective on practice, on your interactions with the teacher, or on what you expect from the practice.

- Do you find that you often speak in ways that control situations with a friend, your children, your spouse, a parent, or a colleague? What would happen if you did not? Give it a try. To begin, pick a person and a relatively low key situation and, for a brief period of time, see if you can find ways to speak that meets the other person and the situation in which you find yourself. For example, if you ask a lot of questions as a way to control, don't. If you tend to gossip to avoid real intimacy, don't. Notice your comfort level with yourself and with the other person.

- Do you teach yoga? If so, consider how you interact with your students. Are you controlling their practice by intimidating them with your authority? Do you consider a student's practice a reflection of your worth as a teacher? Are you allowing each student to mature in his own practice, including developing a yoga that is truly his own? How do you respond when a student does not want to come out of a pose? Or does not want to practice a pose? What feelings arise in you? Perhaps you are more concerned with controlling the class than with teaching it. Are they the same thing for you?

- If you teach yoga, be willing to be a student, too. Can you be in a yoga class and not be in charge? Notice your judgments, especially if things are taught in a style or rhythm that are not yours. Can you accept feedback from another teacher?

- The next time you go on an outing with family or friends, do not be a backseat driver. Assuming that your safety is not at risk, do not comment on the driver's route, speed, or style of driving. Try being a guest.

Mantras for Daily Living
- The only real control I have is the choice of my own thoughts, my own words, and my own actions.

- Control is the greatest illusion.

- What can I let go of right now?

- I can choose how I react. I do not have to react right now.

10

Fear

drishtvemam sva-janam krishna
  yuyutsum samupasthitam

sidanti mama gatrani
  mukham ca parishushyati
vepathush ca sharire me
  romaharshash ca jayate

gandivam sramsate hastat
  tvak caiva paridahyate
na ca shaknomy avasthatum
  bhramativa ca me manah

O Krishna, seeing these my own people standing before me
eager to fight,

my limbs fail, my mouth is parched, trembling lays hold upon my
body, and my hair is caused to bristle with alarm.

My bow slips from my hand, and also my skin is completely afire;
I am also not able to stand, and my mind seems to reel.

—*Bhagavad Gita* 1:28–30

Although you may never actually have to fight for
your life as Arjuna describes in the *Bhagavad Gita,* we all
experience some measure of fear every day. And we have all
felt varying degrees of the bodily manifestations of fear that he
details in book one, verses twenty-eight to thirty: *drishtvemam
sva-janam krishna / yuyutsum samupasthitam / sidanti mama
gatrani / mukham ca parishushyati / vepathush ca sharire me /*

67

romaharshash ca jayate / gandivam sramsate hastat / tvak caiva /
paridahyate / na ca shaknomy avasthatum / bhramativa ca me
manah, or "O Krishna, seeing these my own people standing
before me eager to fight, / my limbs fail, my mouth is parched,
trembling lays hold upon my body, and my hair is caused to
bristle with alarm. / My bow slips from my hand, and also my
skin is completely afire; I am also not able to stand, and my
mind seems to reel."[1]

Most often, the fear that you experience is of short
duration, for example, the sudden jolt that you feel when a car
pulls too close to you on the freeway. Then there is the longer-
lasting fear, such as when you think about your daughter driving
by herself for the first time for that short trip to the store and
back. Sometimes fears are so deep and so persistent that they
are expressed as anxiety or even panic. According to Kathy
Weston, R.N., a nurse practitioner in the Behavioral
Medicine Department at Kaiser Hospital, in Oakland,
California, panic attacks or deep anxiety may be covering up
other life issues, such as alcoholism, a bad marriage or job,
family of origin problems, or old traumas.[2] In other words, the
experience of panic that is attributed to a specific stimulus,
such as public speaking or flying on an airplane, is not the
actual fear. Deep fears of loss have been transferred into fear
of some other object or situation.

Patanjali describes the most pervasive and long-
lasting fear as the fear of death. It is present in all people,
even the wise. He calls it *abhinivesha* in the *Yoga Sutra,*
book two, verses nine and ten: *sva-rasa-vahi vidusho'pi*
tatha-rudho'bhiniveshah / te pratiprasava-heyah sukshmah, or

"The will to live, flowing along by its own momemtum, is rooted thus even in the sages. / These causes of affliction, in their subtle form, are to be overcome by the process of involution."[3]

It is my experience that I feel only two basic emotions: fear and love. However, there are many aspects to each. Take greed, for example. Greed springs from the fear that there isn't enough of whatever you need. Another aspect of fear is anger, which is actually an attempt to defend against a harm that you perceive is coming. One of the most interesting things about fear is that it exists in relationship to the future. Consider this scenario. You are alone at home. You hear an unusual sound coming from the area near a back window. You react with fear: what will happen if an intruder breaks into my house? At another time, you think about the death of a loved one. You feel afraid. Even though it is a given that she will die someday, it has not happened yet—except in your imagination.

It is my experience that when there is actual danger present, I am not afraid. Once I was learning how to drive a small motorcycle that I was hoping to use as transportation to graduate school. It was an old model, and I was just getting up some speed on my first outing when the throttle stuck. I could not stop the motorcycle. I was going to run into a wall. I inventoried the possible solutions, quickly arriving at the only one that made sense at the time. I jumped. Luckily, I was left only with some colorful bruises.

I learned that I would walk to graduate school after all, and learned that I was fearless during the moments when I was actually facing danger. As I discovered, when you are truly present in the moment, even when that moment is life-threatening, you are not afraid. In the verse from the *Bhagavad Gita,* Arjuna is afraid that he may be called upon to act and not of what is happening to him in the moment. If you are involved in actually fighting for your life, there is no time to be afraid. The sympathetic nervous system is mobilizing you to run or attack, and your bodily functions are working full blast. For example, the eyes open wider to see the danger better, blood is shunted to the muscles so that you can use them in the fight, and the mind becomes completely focused on the immediate need at hand. Your nervous system is not distracted by thinking in the abstract about what may happen. Rather, it is dealing with what *is* happening. It is only when you think about what *may* happen or what *could have* happened that you feel afraid.

Is it possible to live without fear? I doubt it and it may not even be desirable. Fear is useful: it warns us of potential danger and has served the human race well as a self-preservation device. In this postmodern era, most of our fears are not about being attacked by wild animals in the woods. Instead, we fear illness, loneliness, and poverty. These, and other fears, either can run our lives or can be viewed as part of our human condition. We can choose to observe our fears on a daily basis and continually bring our awareness back to what is happening in the present moment so that we can live more completely.

Fear Practice

Ms. Weston's advice is that a panic attack will last no more than twenty minutes, and that the most powerful thing we can do is to practice deep breathing and relaxation.[4] These will shift the reactions of the sympathetic nervous system to the parasympathetic nervous system. When activated by the stimulus of a tiger or a thought about a tiger, the sympathetic nervous system causes us to become vigilant and prepared to fight or run. The parasympathetic nervous system does the opposite. Its job is to create an environment in the body that is concerned with growth, repair, digestion, and reproduction— all processes that require the luxury of time.

Whether you suffer from panic attacks or are feeling nervous about a speech that you will give to your colleagues, try this variation of Basic Relaxation Pose (*Shavasana*). Gather together two blankets, a cloth the size of a face towel, and a pillow. Find a quiet place and sit down on the floor, preferably a carpeted one. Fold one blanket into a large rectangle and then roll it. Place the blanket roll under your knees, and cover your feet and legs with the other blanket. Using your elbows for support, slowly lie back. Put the pillow under your head. Bring the blanket up to cover your torso, and place the cloth over your eyes. Finally, tuck your arms under the blanket, palms up.

Feel your torso and arms being supported by the floor and your legs resting completely on the blanket roll. Take several long, slow breaths. All you have to do right now is to be where you are, doing what you are doing. You do not have to solve any problems or meet any demands. Release even more into the support of the floor and blanket roll, with your limbs heavy, your breath slowing, your jaw becoming slack. Lie in this position for five to fifteen minutes.

Come out of Basic Relaxation Pose by slowly bending one knee toward your chest and rolling to lie on one side. Take a couple of breaths before you use your arms to help you come to a sitting position. As you gradually stand up, tell yourself that this feeling of relaxation is always available to you wherever you are. Smile.

Other Practice Suggestions

■ If you are in a situation in which you cannot practice Basic Relaxation Pose, try this exercise. When you become aware of being afraid or anxious, bring your attention to those places in your body where you feel sensations. For many of us, this may be in the throat, the diaphragm, or the stomach. Breathe easily, feeling what arises without judgment or analysis. As you continue to breathe, say out loud to yourself or a trusted friend, "I am feeling afraid." Your willingness to admit that you are afraid can greatly lessen fear's grip on you.

■ This useful exercise was suggested to me when I was growing up. When I fear something, such as giving a speech, calling someone about whether I got a job, or hearing the news a doctor might have about a medical test, I acknowledge my fear before the event. Then I ask myself, What is the worst that can happen? My answer with regard to the speech is that I would make a fool of myself by forgetting my speech or not being able to talk. Then I ask myself, And then what would happen? In the case of giving a speech, I would simply leave the podium, embarrassed but alive. And then what would happen? After I left the podium, my life would go on. Each time I ask, And then what would happen?, it becomes apparent that very soon *nothing* would be happening. This technique has helped me keep many of my fears in perspective. I may still fear giving the speech but that fear no longer controls me completely because I have acknowledged it, felt it, and, in my mind, lived through my worst fear.

Mantras for Daily Living

- And then what would happen?

- Right here, right now.

- I am safe.

- I choose the life that I have right now.

- I am willing to act in the face of fear.

- I can do this.

11

Patience

nirvicara-vaisharadye'adhyatma-prasadah

On attaining the utmost purity of the nirvicara stage of samadhi, there is the dawning of the spiritual light.

—*Yoga Sutra* 1:47

Patience is not mentioned as such by Patanjali in the *Yoga Sutra*. The closest he comes is in book one, verse forty-seven: *nirvicara-vaisharadye'adhyatma-prasadah,*[1] or "On attaining the utmost purity of the nirvicara stage of samadhi, there is the dawning of the spiritual light."[2] *Adhyatma-prasada* mean "calmness, or clarity, of the inner being."[3] Patanjali also mentions *upeksha,* or "equanimity," in book one, verse thirty-three: *maitri-karuna-mudita-upekshanam sukha-duhkha-punya-apunya-vishayanam bhavanatash-citta-prasadanam,* or "The projection of friendliness, compassion, gladness, and equanimity towards objects—be they joyful, sorrowful, meritorious, or demeritorious—bring about the pacification of consciousness."[4] To me, three Sanskrit words quoted—*adhyatma, prasada,* and *upeksha*—convey the feeling of patience. Patanjali teaches that when you enter the stage of perfect wholeness, there is a calmness and a clarity that reflect perfect presence. Many of us have experienced brief snatches of this state. It is that time when we feel perfectly content with whatever is because we feel perfectly connected to whatever is, whether things are going the way we want them or things have fallen apart.

One of the most consistent responses I have to circumstances that I do not like is impatience. I direct this primarily toward myself and sometimes toward family, friends, and even strangers. This pattern must be obvious to those around me, because all of my life I have been admonished, "Be patient." In the past, even though I tried, it did not work. All I was doing was hiding my impatience to be socially acceptable.

When I thought about my impatience, I attributed it to my nature or to the slowness of others. My day of reckoning came while waiting my turn in an airline office in India. I noticed a Western woman who was demanding that something be done "right now." I had been in India for several weeks, and was running on "Indian time" rather than my usual warp speed. I found myself watching this scenario with amusement until I realized that the joke was on me: I had done the same thing so many times. Sometimes I had let it show; other times I had stewed inside.

Right then and there, I decided to pay attention to my impatience. My goal was twofold. First, I was determined to get rid of my impatience. Second, I wanted to become the most patient person in the world. Notice that my good intentions were fraught with impatience! Even so, during the next few weeks, I had a startling realization: There is really no such thing as patience. Let me explain.

I began my patience practice by focusing on those feelings, or bodily sensations, that I experienced whenever I was impatient. Throughout the next several weeks, it seemed that whenever I felt them, I was also out of sync with what was happening. Do you know the phrase, "Go with the flow"? Well, I was doing anything but flowing. I realized that the antidote to impatience was allowing myself to reenter the flow of things, that is, to be in sync with the speed with which things were happening. When I did this, I did not have the feelings, or bodily sensations, that I had been labeling impatience. Reentry began when I recognized my feelings of impatience, and continued as I kept my focus on the feelings of impatience instead of on my thoughts about those feelings.

Next, I practiced noticing my impatient thoughts for several months. When I caught them, they were partnered with another thought: I am wasting time. Buried within this thought was fear, which I will discuss later. What is really wasted? Nothing. All gives me the opportunity to live in the present moment. When I do, I am patient. This realization supports even the most mundane events of my daily life. I can wait in lines, sit in traffic jams, and understand when someone is late for an appointment. All of these times—waiting, sitting, and understanding—are valuable. I can choose not to experience them as wasted time by choosing to be present and actually live these precious moments. After all, to reject them is to reject life itself. The challenge comes in remembering that I can choose and that this choice is the most profound of freedoms.

Carrying on with my practice, I discovered yet another layer of thoughts. Beneath my "time-wasting" thoughts was the most startling realization of all: I was afraid. You see, my self-worth was tied to how much I accomplished. I thought that if I could speed up things around me, then I could get more done. If I did that, then I would be more valued, therefore more loved, and therefore happier. This unconscious fear was so powerful that it had been running my life and affecting my relationships with my family because I would become demanding and pushy.

I felt saddened and yet somehow liberated by these revelations. At last I had some insight into the causes of my impatience. I know I can use the power of my own thoughts to make better choices when I feel impatience creeping in. I no longer wish to get rid of impatience, but to pay attention to the thoughts and feelings that underlie it. Whenever I can, I choose thoughts of letting go so that I can ease back into the moment. I find a phrase from *The Ten Second Miracle: Creating Relationship Breakthroughs,* by Gay Hendricks, to be a helpful reminder: "to be in an easeful flow of love and connection in our lives."[5] Sometimes I even say part of it out loud to help myself choose what I really want in my life. I doubt that I will ever be able to live without feeling impatient. But now I am more able to choose to respond in a different way. It may seem like a small step, but for me it is profound.

Patience Practice

You can use your yoga practice as a way to explore your relationship to patience. For example, pick a seated yoga pose, such as Lotus Pose (*Padmasana*), Sage Pose (*Siddhasana*), or Seated Mountain Pose (*Tadasana,* variation) that you can hold for two to three minutes. You can practice this pose alone or after Basic Relaxation Pose (*Shavasana*) at the end of your regular yoga routine. Once you are comfortable and settled, bring your attention to where you feel the breath in your body. From that place, follow the movement of each inhalation and each exhalation. Notice what arises. Are you bored? Waiting for the time to pass? Drifting to thoughts of the past or the future? Can you bring yourself back, time and again, to the movement of the breath? Notice, too, the more pleasant experiences, such as calmness, clarity, and equanimity. Whether pleasant or unpleasant, can you contain your experiences?

Does the focus of the breath move? Are you more comfortable with it in one place than another? Does the breath have texture? Is it smooth or rough? Dry or moist? Slow or fast? Can you feel the breath in both the front body and the back body? Can you rest in the present moment, even if it is just for one inhalation and one exhalation of breath?

Gradually increase the time that you hold the pose until you reach ten minutes. What happens to your bodily and mental comfort level? Does your internal alarm clock go off at the time you used to end practice? Do you want to stay longer? Just stay with whatever arises. (Practice note: You should not feel any numbness or tingling in the arms or legs. If you do, come out of the pose. Next time, prop yourself differently, and stay for a shorter time.)

To conclude practice, open your eyes, stretch your arms and legs, and walk slowly around the room before resuming your normal activities.

Other Practice Suggestions

- Just for fun, choose the longest line at the bank or the grocery store. Breathe slowly and pay attention to your bodily sensations. Your willingness to focus on your impatience will eventually reconnect you with the reality that everything is moving at the proper speed.

- Take a walk. If the walking surface is appropriate, you can even take off your shoes and socks. Find your own pace, neither pushing to get somewhere nor pulling back. Feel the surface beneath your feet, the air around you, and your bodily sensations. You might find that your natural pace is a lot slower than you had thought. Notice your comfort level when you find that pace. Most of all, enjoy your walk!

- The next time that your spouse, child, or friend is upset, listen to her with your full attention. Do not make any comments or offer any advice. Let her know in advance that you will be practicing compassionate listening. Stay focused on her for as long as it takes.

- If your spouse, child, or friend wants to explain something that is important to him, but not necessarily interesting to you, listen attentively. Consciously relax your body and breathe slowly.

- When you feel yourself becoming impatient, remember that whatever the present situation, it will change. The traffic jam will clear, your teenager will mature, your messy house eventually will be cleaned. Even the most difficult of life's situations will not remain the same. If you can remember this, you will be more likely to recognize solutions when they present themselves.

Mantras for Daily Living
- Everything is moving at the proper speed.

- Choice is the most profound freedom.

- It won't always be like this.

- There is always enough time in nature.

- Is the problem the situation, or is it my reaction to the situation?

12

Attachment and Aversion

sukha-anushayi ragah
duhkha-anushayi dveshah

Attachment is that which rests on pleasant experiences.
Aversion is that which rests on sorrowful experiences.

—*Yoga Sutra* 2:7–8

One morning, as I was sipping my hot drink and reading the paper, a *Calvin and Hobbes* cartoon caught my attention. Calvin is a rambunctious six-year-old, and Hobbes is his tiger. He is a stuffed tiger, but to Calvin and the reader, he is real. In this particular strip, Hobbes comes upon Calvin sitting in serene repose. Calvin tells Hobbes that he has discovered the meaning of life, explaining that everyone was put on Earth to do exactly what he, Calvin, wants, and when they discover that, they will be happy and will have meaning in their lives, too.[1] I cut out the cartoon and posted it on our family communications center, the refrigerator.

For something to be funny, it has to have an element of truth: lies are not funny. So when I find myself laughing, I try to figure out what's true for me. I resonate with Calvin because I, too, secretly yearn for everyone to do what I want! I think that we all feel this way. Here's an example. You are going to the bank. In your mind, this *should* occur by your car starting easily and all traffic moving out of your way. There *should* be a parking place right in front, with time on the meter. Further, you *should* be able to go into the bank and conduct your business with no waiting. The teller *should* be polite, accurate, and even know your name. These improbable expectations are somehow lodged in the back of your mind so that when reality intrudes, such as the car doesn't start, or there is a lot of traffic, or there is no parking place, you become frustrated, irritated, or even angry. At this moment, you are reacting to the way you think something *should* be and not the way things actually *are*.

Patanjali offers two important concepts that speak directly to this point in book two, verses seven and eight, in his *Yoga Sutra: sukha-anushayi ragah / duhkha-anushayi dveshah,* or "Attachment is that which rests on pleasant experiences. Aversion is that which rests on sorrowful experiences."[2] *Raga,* or "attachment," and *dvesha,* or "aversion," are two of the five *klesha,* or "impediments,"[3] that we face in becoming whole. (The other kleshas are ignorance, egoism, and fear of death.[4]) Although attachment and aversion seem to be opposites, they are actually the same thing.

In daily life, you are constantly pulled between trying to get what you want and trying to avoid what you don't want. Whether you are busy pulling something in or pushing it away, there is a relationship between you and the object or event that limits your freedom. Here are three examples. First, someone who overeats and someone who is anorexic are both attached to food. One is positively attached and thinks about how to get more; the other is negatively attached and thinks about how to avoid it. Second, if you love someone, you think about her all the time. If you hate someone, you think about her all the time. Finally, if you have a rough spot on your tooth, your tongue is always rubbing the tooth. The roughness is attractive to the tongue even though it is not something that you want. And when you get your teeth cleaned, your tongue continually moves over that smoothness because you find it pleasurable and want to feel it over and over again.

All day long, you react to things going right and things going wrong. I use a Mantra for Daily Living to help me remember that I am getting caught in this incessant push-pull. One of my favorites is actually a question: How *should* it be? I say this to myself and sometimes even out loud. When I do, I can more easily see my attachment or aversion to the outcome of some event. In addition, it helps me to remember that things are the way they are, and that I have a choice about whether I want to be in reaction to how they are. In short, I have a choice about whether I will be controlled by attachment and by aversion.

I am not suggesting that you do not have preferences about the way things go. Having a preference is natural: vanilla instead of chocolate, the blue shirt instead of the red, this college instead of that one. Attachment is the process which occurs in the body-mind when you do not get your preference; aversion is a form of attachment. Both create bodily and emotional reactions. Aversion may create frustration, anger, and blame of self or others. I find that fear is often at the root of my reactions when I am in a state of aversion. Clinging to a preference, whether it is from attachment or aversion, creates suffering. It is also the precise moment when you can grow by choosing to recognize attachment or aversion for what it is.

The sad thing about being caught up in attachment or aversion is that it interferes with the ability to experience things as they are. Even when these things are painful and difficult, there is an advantage to fully experiencing them as they occur. When you do, you are unburdened. You do not have to carry it with you in an unfinished state. This process of experiencing the difficulty *now* allows you to begin to heal. Learning to live in the moment, complete with your preferences and recognizing attachment and aversion, is like a soothing balm on a sunburn.

Attachment and Aversion Practice

One day, I decided to count the number of times that I became irritated or frustrated throughout the day. I do not mean angry, but just irritated at the way things were going. I kept track on a hand-held counter. I was shocked at the total: sixty-seven times that day I sent my nervous system into action over things of small consequence.

"How *should* it be?," a Mantra of Daily Living, is a powerful practice. I suggest that you say it for the next several days (or longer) when you feel yourself caught in either attachment or aversion. It can remind you that things are as they are and that you have the freedom to react or not. I have gradually learned to value the awareness that it brings me.

Other Practice Suggestions

■ A friend told me that at the end of each day on a meditation retreat, she wrote down one- or two-word phrases to describe the various mind states she had experienced during the day. For example, clinging, joyful, angry, happy, self-indulgent, repetitious, sad, tired, bored, and so on. To get a look at your mind states, write them down at the end of the next three days, using attachment and aversion as the categories in which to put your descriptions. The purpose is not to make a journal of your experiences or to be judgmental, but to quickly note what you remember. At the end of the three days, notice the repetitions, what you classify as attachment and as aversion, and what arose when you were alone as opposed to when you were interacting with others.

■ Based on what you uncovered in the preceding exercise, pick one mind state. Let's say that you select tired mind. For the next several days, pay particular attention to the arising and falling away of that mind state. Does it present itself as attachment or as aversion? Is it sometimes one and then the other? What are your bodily sensations when you are pulling something toward you? What are they when you are pushing something away? Is tired mind the manifestation of having been doing too much? If so, are these things that you even want to do? Is tired mind a way to numb yourself? Do you notice it arise when you are with particular people or in particular circumstances? Most important is not to judge yourself as good or bad, right or wrong. Just notice.

■ Think about some daily task that you dislike, perhaps taking out the garbage, making the bed, or returning phone calls. Pick something that you regularly need to do but regularly avoid. Then do this task faithfully for the next twenty-one days. Notice how or if your attitude changes. Keep it going. Pick another task and do the same thing.

■ A similar practice can work for learning about attachment.

Pick something that you feel that you need to do, and let it slide. For example, I like making my bed first thing, so that the bedroom is orderly. Now I sometimes actually do not make the bed all day! Another example is my incessant need to pick up. Now on some Sundays, I leave the newspaper scattered on the living room floor all day long. I must admit that it takes a bit of remembering to use my attachment to neatness and order as a practice point. You try it.

Mantras for Daily Living

- How *should* it be?

- Things are as they are, and I have a choice about how I react to them.

- What will happen if I don't get what I want right now?

- This is just a thought.

- Will this be important in a year? Five years?

13

Suffering

heyam duhkham-anagatam
That which is to be overcome is sorrow yet to come.
—*Yoga Sutra* 2:16

Distinguished physiologist Arthur C. Guyton, M.D., reports that the sensations of pleasure and pain, controlled in large part by the hypothalamus in the brain, greatly affect our behavior.[1] This can help us understand why we make so many of the choices we do. Understandably, we act in ways that we hope will help us avoid pain or punishment, and maximize pleasure or reward.

There are many types of pain. For example, a few years ago a friend was locked in a nasty custody fight with her ex-husband over her teenage daughter. We had a number of talks about her painful predicament. One day, she came to see me. She was serene: all the stress had drained from her face. She told me that she had realized that her daughter would be fine with her ex-husband and that she had decided not to fight for custody.

This was a great teaching for me. The lesson I learned was the difference between pain and suffering. As I discussed in Chapter One, "Spiritual Seeking," physical, emotional, and mental pain are inevitable in life. Suffering is another matter. Suffering is the personalization we bring to our difficulties. For example, we blame others for our pain, or we feel sorry for ourselves because of the pain. My friend was in pain about her daughter, and she was suffering with the situation. She had no control over the actions of another, but she did have control over her own reactions to them. Once she accepted that her daughter would be fine with her ex-husband, she chose to let go of the power struggle with him and, consequently, gained strength and serenity.

Patanjali gives us an important clue about suffering in his *Yoga Sutra,* book two, verse sixteen: *heyam duhkham-anagatam,* or "That which is to be overcome is sorrow yet to come."[2] Here, he teaches that we can choose to suffer or not to suffer. Obviously, the suffering of the past cannot be wiped out, and the suffering of this moment is what I am experiencing now. But the suffering that exists in the future can be avoided by the choices that I make now.

This teaching bespeaks great hope. But how are we to avoid the suffering that is yet to come? The *Yoga Sutra* offers advice in book two, verse five: *anitya-ashuci-duhkha-anatmasu nitya-shuci-sukha-atma-khyatir-avidya,* or "Nescience is the seeing of that which is eternal, pure, joyful, and the Self in that which is ephemeral, impure, sorrowful, and the non-self."[3] In other words, we suffer because of the process of identifying with the pain. If we have an internal dialogue that reinforces the belief that we are suffering, that we have no choice, that the whole world is doing it to us, then we will remain stuck in our suffering. The paradox about suffering is that no one can make us suffer. We can choose to feel left out, incompetent, or inferior. Others may act in unkind ways. But there is no way that we will feel left out, incompetent, or inferior unless we participate in the process. Although we may have feelings about what is happening to us, whether we suffer is up to us. It is a matter of choice.

Another interesting idea about suffering is that it does not come out of nowhere. Referring to one of the states of suffering in book two, verse four, of the *Yoga Sutra*, Patanjali writes, *avidya kshetram uttaresham prasupta-tanu-vicchinna-udaranam,* or "Nescience is the field of the other causes of affliction; they can be dormant, attenuated, intercepted, or aroused."[4] Here, *prasupta,* or "dormant," describes how some roots of our suffering may be in the unconscious. However, when events occur in a specific way, this suffering may suddenly move into awareness. An example of this dormant suffering can be seen in the relationship of partners or spouses. In the beginning, everything seems to go so well that we say that we are "in love." After some time, difficulties invariably arise, seemingly out of nowhere. Actually, the difficulties were there from the beginning or they could not surface.

In its broadest sense, yoga practice is about inviting what is unconscious to the surface so that it can be integrated into conscious awareness. An example of this is what happens when you practice yoga poses. In forward bends, it may become apparent that there is tightness in the backs of the legs. There may be a combination of causes for the tightness, including physical and emotional. Several reactions are possible. You can blame yourself for being so tight; you can blame the pose for being so hard; or you can blame the teacher for making you do the pose. Neither the pose nor the teacher are creating the difficulty. The difficulty was there all along. The yoga pose just gives you a chance to experience it and, it is hoped, release it.

Our intimate relationships are shaped by our suffering. It is the process of unmasking this suffering that helps us to grow, to achieve true intimacy with others, and to live fully. According to Patanjali, the future is bright. The choice to embrace it is ours.

Suffering Practice

This practice will help you observe the differences between thinking and obsessing. Begin by finding a quiet place and time, and write down your ten most frequent thoughts. Do not worry if you cannot find ten. Review them. If you are like me, most of these thoughts are obsessions. Obsessing does not deal with reality, and usually increases my suffering.

An example: My husband is late coming home from work. I have two choices. The first is to observe that fact, and decide when and if action is necessary. The second is to obsess, spinning thought after thought to interpret why he is late. My mind could run to a thousand "what ifs," always imagining the worst: He was injured. He has left me. Although I might eventually have to face the pain that something dreadful had actually happened to him or that he had left me, I do not have to inflict suffering upon myself by spinning my thoughts.

The next time that your thoughts are spinning, gently bring your awareness to a bodily sensation, such as the feeling of the backs of your legs against a chair, the tightness in your belly, or your feet resting on the floor. What you feel in your body is right here, right now. If you notice your mind moving back to repeating thoughts, bring your awareness back to your body. Give the sensation your undivided attention. When you do, it will begin to change.

Other Practice Suggestions

- Pick one area of your life, for example, your physical health. For a week, make new choices in the now that support future health. These could be eating whole grains, going to bed earlier, avoiding watching the news immediately before bedtime, taking a morning walk, or a combination of choices. At the end of the week, notice how you feel, physically and emotionally. Appreciate yourself for your new choices.

- If you practice yoga poses, pick one that you can do fairly easily. Without harming yourself, hold this pose for twice as long as you normally do. Notice your inner dialogue when the pose becomes uncomfortable. Do you blame the pose, yourself, or me for your suffering? Do you want out? Consider that perhaps your suffering comes from your attitude and not from the sensations themselves.

- The next time that you are upset, notice your physiological responses, such as increased tension in your muscles, changes in your breath, and tightness in your belly. How much time during the day do you spend in this state? Is this the way you want to spend your life? Choose to let go of suffering in this very moment.

Mantras for Daily Living

- Who is suffering?

- I can release all suffering and live life right now.

- Life may be difficult, but I do not need to suffer.

- This is part of it, too.

14

Impermanence

anitya-ashuci-duhkha-anatmasu nitya-shuci-sukha-
atma-khyatir avidya

Nescience is the seeing of that which is eternal, pure, joyful
and the Self in that which is ephemeral, impure, sorrowful,
and the non-self.

—*Yoga Sutra* 2:5

Some years ago, I had the chance to return to my
childhood home. I was so excited as my car turned onto the
once-familiar street that had been my world. Initially, I was
startled by how big the trees had gotten. As I walked down
the sidewalks, where I had learned to skate and spent hours
playing hopscotch, I was struck by how small and close
together everything seemed. Later, reflecting on my trip of
remembrance, I realized that I had had expectations that the
old neighborhood would be just the same as when I left it.
Although intellectually I knew that change is constant and
that it affects everyone and everything, I had not applied this
principle to myself. In my mind, it was only other people's
neighborhoods that changed: mine remained fixed.

According to Shakyamuni Buddha, the very nature of
reality is impermanence. Everything is in a state of flux.
Patanjali echoes this wisdom in book two, verse five, of his
Yoga Sutra: anitya-ashuci-duhkha-anatmasu nitya-shuci-
sukha-atma-khyatir avidya, or "Nescience is the seeing of that
which is eternal, pure, joyful and the Self in that which is

ephemeral, impure, sorrowful, and the non-self."[1] He defines
an aspect of *avidya* ("nescience") as mistaking the noneternal
for the eternal. Simply put, when we think that we (or the
people and things that we love) will remain the same, we do
not understand impermanence.

Is anything permanent? We can look to nature to
teach us. Consider the cycle of the seasons: The ices of winter
give way to the burst of spring buds. Summer brings heat and
dust, followed by golden leaves and the chill of autumn.
Consider the changes in the structure of the Earth: Mountain
ranges are pushed up by the Earth's changing crust, and
islands are formed by volcanic eruptions. All is subject to
erosion by the elements. Quantum physics teaches us about
the uncertainty and impermanence of the very stuff of which
the world is made. The distinction between waves and particles
is blurred, and each behaves like the other. They live in a cloud
of possibilities. The very building blocks of our universe are
ephemeral and not the lasting things that we may think. Every
day, all day, our bodies engage in impermanence with each
breath. Your current inhalation is unlike any other you have
ever taken. At its fullness, it surrenders to the exhalation, itself
different from the one preceding it.

As I described in Chapter Three, "Letting Go," one
day I was filling out a form that asked for my permanent
address and whether I owned my home. I may live in the
San Francisco Bay Area now, but where is my home after I
die? And don't I need permanent possession of something to
own it? It appears that I am renting everything for this lifetime,
including my body, my family, my education and knowledge,

my experiences, and my ATM card. Nothing is truly mine. To answer the question I asked in the preceding text, Nothing is permanent except impermanence.

Shakyamuni Buddha summarized impermanence in The Five Remembrances. They are presented by Thich Nhat Hanh, a Vietnamese Zen Buddhist monk and author of *Being Peace,* in *The Plum Village Chanting Book:*

1. I am of the nature to grow old. There is no way to escape growing old.

2. I am of the nature to have ill health. There is no way to escape having ill health.

3. I am of the nature to die. There is no way to escape death.

4. All that is dear to me and everyone I love are of the nature to change. There is no way to escape being separated from them.

5. My actions are my only true belongings. I cannot escape the consequences of my actions. My actions are the ground on which I stand.[2]

At first glance, this could be taken as a grim list of what we will lose. I see it as a loving reminder of the life we have been given. As such, everything *is* perfect. Along with things that surely will be lost, impermanence makes way for new possibilities, such as working out a difficulty with a friend, giving birth to a child after years of trying to conceive, recovering from an illness, learning to do a yoga pose that you thought once was beyond your ability, and more.

It takes a brave heart to deeply accept that everything changes. Even when things are not the way we want them, we still fear change. Our attachment to things remaining the same creates suffering. When we cling to the illusion of permanence, what we actually hope to secure is protection from the terrifying unknown that impermanence may represent.

When I asked my husband for his comments on how to observe impermanence, he replied ruefully, "Have children." We both laughed. Seriously, I am not advocating having children in order to practice! However, relationships of all kinds are a perfect backdrop against which to observe our ideas about attachment to permanence.

As babies, our children were slow to establish a routine of eating and sleeping. I was seriously invested in having a schedule. Just when they would finally settle into a pattern and I could make plans for my day, their rhythms would change. It took me a long time to recognize my attachment, and I did two things to help myself. First, I accepted that my babies' choice of nap time was not pre-dictable. Second, I created some predictability for myself by hiring a babysitter for the same two hours every day. Although things around me continued to change, at least I knew that I could count on those two hours—except when that changed because the babysitter could not come!

I remember returning from teaching an out-of-state yoga workshop many years ago. My husband and children picked me up at the airport. I was shocked to observe that our daughter had actually grown during the weekend. Then there are the teen years. We make plans with our kids, only to have those plans change half a dozen times in one afternoon as they (and we) shift to accommodate their friends. Learning to let go of my attachment to things remaining the same strikes an even deeper chord within me as the children undergo the fascinating metamorphosis into adults before my eyes. Someday the child-parent relationship may reverse. As I age, they may become my helpers, health care advisers, or financial consultants.

When a yoga teacher was asked about permanence in marriage, he replied, "Do you want permanence in your marriage? Then marry a dead man." Like all relationships, marriage is a work in progress. However, we expect our marriage (and other intimate relationships) to remain unchanged. When I married, I had a set of expectations, including that this relationship would fulfill all my needs for intimacy. Now I recognize that, as one of life's vicissitudes, marriage changes—in my case, from romantically charged lust, to deep friendship, to spiritual partnership.

If you find yourself thinking that there must be some things that are permanent, write them down. Take your time. If you find any, please write to me! Remember impermanence when things go badly, so that you will not be overly burdened by your troubles. And remember it especially when things go well, so that you will be present enough to cherish the sweet moments of your life.

Impermanence Practice

Find a plant in your garden, outside your office, or in a nearby park that you can visit each day in the next week. If you cannot get out, is there one that you can see out your window? What do you notice from day to day? Are the flowers cycling from bud to bloom? Has it lost some leaves? Or sprouted new ones? Anything else? What do you notice about your relationship with the plant throughout? After the week is done, check back every so often to see how the plant is faring.

Other Practice Suggestions

- Memorize The Five Remembrances. Say them to yourself each morning and evening.

- There are other ways in which you can work with The Five Remembrances. For example, as your children leave for school or as you part from a friend, recall the following: "All that is dear to me and everyone I love are of the nature to change. There is no way to escape being separated from them."[3] If you are having a disagreement with your partner, before speaking, try to remember, "My actions are my only true belongings. I cannot escape the consequences of my actions. My actions are the ground on which I stand."[4]

- Make a list of the things about your life that have changed in the past three months. Whether they are major or minor, it is important that you do not judge them as good or bad. Just notice what has changed. For example, a yoga pose has become easier to do; hair has grayed; you have read a new book by a favorite author; or you have celebrated a birthday. Keep your list and review it in three months, just before you make a new list.

- Make a list of the things about your relationships that have changed in the past three months. For example, you have resolved a problem with your child; an issue with your spouse that you thought was resolved that has arisen as unfinished; you have reached a new understanding with a coworker; or you find that you are relating to an old friend in a new way.

Mantras for Daily Living

- Nothing is permanent except impermanence.

- It won't always be like this.

- When I accept change, I accept life.

- Change is not a mistake: it is all there is.

- I embrace change and let go of fear.

- I put my faith in the permanence of change.

- Letting go of the past revitalizes today.

PART THREE

Embracing All Life: Yoga in the World

15

Greed

ye hi samsparshaja bhoga
  duhkha-yonaya eva te
adyantavantah kaunteya
  na teshu ramate budhah

For the contact-born enjoyments are wombs of sorrow,
having a beginning and an end. In these, O son of Kunti,
the sage does not delight.

—*Bhagavad Gita* 5:22

Years ago, a situation presented itself to me as the perfect opportunity to teach my three children (and myself) about greed. It all began on a Wednesday night as I was leaving to teach my yoga classes. I told the baby-sitter that after dinner the children could have the apple pie that I had purchased at the health food store earlier in the day. This was indeed a big treat. Neither my husband nor I like sweets very much, so we rarely have them around. When I returned, the children were asleep. The baby-sitter told me that there had been a huge fight about the pie. Not only did each child want more pie, but equally intolerable to all three was the possibility that one might get more pie than another.

Needless to say, I was dismayed. By the time the next Wednesday rolled around, I had purchased not one, but *three* apple pies. Before leaving to teach, I told the children that after dinner each child could have his or her very own apple pie. I stressed that, even if they started eating apple pie at that moment and did nothing else for twenty-four hours a day for the rest of their lives, there would still be apple pies left in the world for them to eat. I wanted them to realize that there is enough time, enough love, and certainly enough apple pie in life.

The baby-sitter looked at me in amazement. I told her that I believed that the cause of many of the world's ills could be directly connected to greed, and that I thought that it was crucial that children learn from an early age that there is enough of what they need. I wanted my children to be free of the fear that creates greed. (Although it is certainly true that the distribution of the world's resources is unequal, I do believe that there *is* enough *if* we conserve and treat the Earth with respect.) The long-term effect of my approach, I believe, has been healthy for my children. As they have grown up, they have progressively shown signs of experiencing the joy that comes from giving. When I remind them of the pie incident, they grin and understand its importance.

Yoga's sacred texts directly address greed. Patanjali counsels us to practice *aparigraha*, or "greedlessness,"[1] in three different verses of book two of his *Yoga Sutra*. First, there is verse twenty-nine: *yama-niyama-asana-pranayama-pratyahara-dharana-dhyana-samadhayo' shtav-angani*, or "Restraint, observance, posture, breath-control, sense-withdrawal, concentration, meditative-absorption, and enstasy are the eight members of yoga."[2] Next, there is verse thirty: *ahimsa-satya-asteya-brah-macarya-aparigraha yamah*, or "Non-harming, truthfulness, non-stealing, chastity, and greedlessness are the restraints."[3] Finally, there is verse thirty-nine: *aparigraha-sthairye janma-kathamta-sambodhah*, or "When steadied in greedlessness, he secures knowledge of the wherefore of his birth(s)."[4]

In book five, verse twenty-two, the *Bhagavad Gita* presents the great irony of greed: *ye hi samsparshaja bhoga / duhkha-yonaya eva te / adyantavantah kaunteya / na teshu ramate budhah,* or "For the contact-born enjoyments are wombs of sorrow, having a beginning and an end. In these, O son of Kunti, the sage does not delight."[5] True enough, but how are we to live lives of greedlessness?

I think that we begin by understanding greed, especially what motivates our own seemingly greedy behavior. Greed presents itself as the longing for both the material and the nonmaterial, especially wanting more than is needed. However, whatever you stockpile—be it diamonds, big houses, fame, money, proficiency at advanced yoga poses, or less flashy things, you will inevitably enounter two certainties. First (as discussed in Chapter Fourteen, "Impermanence"), all will be lost. Second, these things, in and of themselves, will never satisfy your cravings, which are expressions of your feelings of fear and emptiness. You see, sometimes we temporarily lose our way, becoming convinced that if we acquire this thing or that skill, we will finally become acceptable to ourselves and to the world. In our fear, we have forgotten that we are already whole.

My husband and I were markedly unsuccessful at teaching our young children not to be greedy about their toys. No matter how reasonably we presented our case, we met resistance and tears. We finally hit upon a successful strategy: the twenty-four-hour rule. This meant that when the kids received new Christmas or birthday goodies, they did not have to share their loot for the first twenty-four hours. After that time, they were asked to share, especially when the owner was not playing with the toy. We found that this rule worked well. It opened the door to contentment, as it soothed their fears of scarcity and loss, of having an enemy, and of feeling powerless over something that was supposed to belong to them.

A friend once translated a Chinese expression for me: "Have you eaten to contentment?" This seems a powerful orientation to satiating hunger, be it for food or anything else. It calls on us to shift our focus from filling an emptiness to experiencing contentment. With this shift comes the possibility of practicing nongreed. When we seek contentment, or what Patanjali calls *samtosha,* we are closer to experiencing our own wholeness. In book two, verse forty-two, he writes, *samtosad-anuttamah sukha-labhah,* or "Through contentment unexcelled joy is gained."[6]

But how do you shift your focus? All religious traditions admonish us not to steal, not to take what is not given. I agree wholeheartedly. However, what about learning to take what *is* given, whether pleasant or painful? I propose that you begin this "contentment shift" by deeply accepting and having gratitude for all that is given: the breakfast that you ate this morning, oceans and rivers, the yoga poses that you have learned to practice, sunshine and sky, freedom of speech, mountains, your cat, bananas, love, a backache, the moon, the yoga poses that you are unable to do, prairie grasses, your family, clouds and rain, your most recent vacation, California poppies, the death of a friend, stars, your work, wind, apple pie, and your breath. Can you see the endless possibilities of what you have been given? Can you see in each the reflection of your own wholeness?

Contentment asks for only one thing: that you truly live in the experience of the moment. With contentment comes a lessening of fear. And with this comes the ability to share the most important thing that you have been given: your love, your wholeness.

Contentment Practice

You can train yourself to be aware of your impulses toward greed. Whenever you find yourself feeling greedy about time, food, love, or something else, I suggest that you practice this Mantra for Daily Living: There is always enough. You can say it either to yourself or out loud. As you do, invite contentment into your heart.

Other Practice Suggestions

- Make your own list of what strikes you about the life that you have been given. If you'd like, you can develop your "contentment muscle" by keeping the list going. Add to the list every day or however often works best for you.

- Return what you borrow; give away what you really do not need.

- Eat only when you feel hungry.

- The twenty-four hour rule for adults: The next time you have a craving for a new material good, wait at least twenty-four hours before you buy it.

- For the next three days, stop eating at exactly the moment that you feel full.

- Make a list of the material things that you would like to have. Prioritize the items in their order of importance to you. Whenever you have the urge to buy something, consult your list and follow it. Ask yourself, How will this new thing enrich my life?, and What are the costs and benefits I would derive from owning this new thing?

Mantras for Daily Living

- I live with contentment.

- I am filled by the life that I have been given.

- There is always enough.

- I can't be greedy and grateful at the same time.

- What can I be grateful for right now?

16

Service

tasmad asaktah satatam
karyam karma samacara
asakto hy acaran karma
param apnoti purushah

Therefore always perform unattached the deed to be done.
For the man who performs action without attachment obtains
the Supreme.

—*Bhagavad Gita* 3:19

Whether we are engaging in social action or helping a
friend move to a new apartment on a Saturday afternoon, we
are all inspired to serve the needs of others. So important is
service that it has its own name within the system of yoga:
karma yoga, or "self-transcending action." When we practice
karma yoga, we engage our deep connection with others and
with life itself. In book three, verse nineteen, the *Bhagavad Gita*
teaches us an important aspect of service: *tasmad asaktah*
satatam / karyam karma samacara / asakto hy acaran karma /
param apnoti purushah, or "Therefore always perform unattached the deed to be done. For the man who performs action
without attachment obtains the Supreme."[1]

When my daughter was being interviewed for acceptance into a high school, she was told that they were consider-
ing making community service mandatory. The interviewer
asked what she thought about this. My daughter replied that
if community service were to become a required subject, its
purpose would be defeated. For her, the point was for the

students to choose the option of community service. I couldn't agree more and, as it turned out, so did the interviewer.

Choice is the heart of service. You can serve the world by doing small, unsung actions each day without much difficulty. To name a few: pick up a piece of glass on the sidewalk so that no one cuts herself; carry away the trash on a hiking trail; move to another seat on a bus so that a family can sit together; and donate your children's discarded toys to a shelter. Although important, they neither require significant interaction with another person nor the energy it takes to honor those relationships. You may have a heartfelt desire to volunteer at the hospital, or to help your children with their homework after you have had a long day, or to listen when a friend telephones with a problem. At the same time, you may be on overload and feel resentful at being called into service. Is it possible to follow Patanjali's lead and serve without attachment to outcome, including how you should appear to others? How do you honor the spirit of karma yoga and also honor your own needs?

A friend and I were once discussing the incredible demands of motherhood. In truth, I was complaining about how little time I had for myself because I was almost always doing something for someone else. She explained how she lost her way when her actions were only for others and she forgot about herself. I mulled over her words for a long time. I even felt anger at her point of view, probably because it did not align with what I thought was yogic. It took me a long time to understand her wisdom.

To begin, it is important to acknowledge the complexity of our motivation to help either when asked or because the desire has spontaneously arisen. It may be difficult for us to know competely why we do what we do. But one thing is certain: all of our feelings are part of our humanness, including our resentments and our disillusionments. My friend understood that although motherhood is demanding, it does not demand that she be selfless. It is, in fact, quite the opposite: to parent well, she really must take care of herself.

Following her lead, you can come to karma yoga by determining what is possible for you right here and right now. You can assess your physical health, energy level, and abilities. You can say no if that is more truthful than a resentful yes. You can notice when you get internal messages that you are helping in order to gain power, or recognition, or love. As challenging as it may be to embrace these parts of yourself, you can be grateful for having been given the opportunity to see yourself and your situation more clearly. Just as in asana practice, when you bring the wandering mind back to the movement of the breath or the sensations of the body, so too you can check in with yourself—time and again—to make sure, as my friend taught me, that you have not lost your way. When you serve yourself, you make it possible to serve others. And when you serve others, you acknowledge your interdependence with all of life.

Service Practice

You have the opportunity to serve all day long: at home with the children, at the office with your fellow workers, at the yoga studio with your students. The question is, What kind of servant are you: resentful and manipulative, or joyful and inspiring? A simple way to practice service is to find something around your home or work that needs doing and to do it without fanfare. Do not tell anyone that you are going to do it, and do not talk about it afterward. Try to pick a "service project" every day or at least once a week.

Other Practice Suggestions

- After you have worked with the Service Practice several times, notice what opportunities to serve come your way. Perhaps there is something in your neighborhood, or at your children's school, or at your place of worship. If it is a big project, enlist the aid of a friend or two. Begin by stating your intention to yourself, such as, I will do what I can in response to what is needed here. Pay attention to your thoughts after you have completed the project. Are you waiting for someone to thank you or give you recognition? If you are thanked, accept it.

- If you regularly volunteer and feel burned out, maybe you need a break. Take it. Then reassess what is possible for you: How much? And how often?

- If you teach yoga (or anything else), notice if your teaching is aligned with the spirit of karma yoga. Do you take care of your physical, mental, and emotional needs so that you are prepared to teach? Is your practice stale: are you teaching by rote? Do you sometimes call attention to yourself when it is not necessary? Do you call it "my" yoga class and forget that it is also the students' yoga class? Is teaching a job, or an act of service, or both?

■ I like to say that I teach for myself and practice for my students. What I mean by this is that although I certainly pay attention to the needs of the students, I teach what is in my heart. I try to let go of my fears that I might not be teaching what they want or in a manner that pleases every-one. Instead, I offer the teaching as my gift. In order not to get too impressed with my performance of an advanced pose or too depressed about my physical limitations, I try to focus on my personal practice as a learning experience that will allow me to share yoga more purely with my students. This attitude helps me to remember to teach and practice in the spirit of service. The next time that you practice, ask yourself, Whom am I serving now? If you teach yoga, ask yourself the same question.

Mantras for Daily Living

■ I will do what I can in response to what is needed here.

■ I can serve myself without feeling guilty.

■ Everyone works in the "service industry."

■ Helping others means helping myself.

■ Whom am I serving now?

17

Connection

na tv evaham jatu nasam
  na tvam neme janadhipah
na caiva bhavishyamah
  sarve vayam atah param

Verily, never was I not, were you not, or were these rulers not, nor will any one of us not be henceforth.

—*Bhagavad Gita* 2:12

It is my experience that the most powerful human drive is the one for connection. It is keenly apparent from the moment of birth when baby and mother make their connection through touch and the breast. It is apparent in the hand-holding of eight-year-old girls who are best friends, as well as in the rough-and-tumble play of young boys who are inseparable. It is even evident in the seemingly rude comments of adult male friends who chide each other about an ugly tie or a favorite sports team's loss over the weekend.

Even though we may not always know how to express our yearning for connection, nonetheless, we long for it—with other humans and with that Mystery we call God, or the Universe, or the Source. We long for this connection because we feel incomplete without the meaning it provides in our lives. This driving need shapes our lives, in ways large—such as marriage—and small—such as a lunch date between friends. Although we may, at times, feel disconnected, we can rest in the certainty that all beings, all things, are interconnected. A dramatic example of this is the night sky. Twinkling against a net of inky black are billions of stars. It takes each one to make our solar system. When I was in physical therapy school, we learned in anatomy class about the blood vessels in different parts of the body. One day, I realized that there is really only one blood vessel and that it takes on different characteristics depending on where it is. Look at your hand. Tell me, is this structure a single unit or a palm and five fingers? Whether you see the separateness of the stars, or blood vessels, or your palm and fingers, or whether you see the oneness of the sky, the vascular system, or your hand depends on your perception. And perception depends on what I call the grid.

You, like all other humans, have a grid that separates you from life. This grid is formed by your beliefs about the world and yourself, and by your experiences and your reactions to them. Whatever filters through, you call reality. But is it? Ask a roomful of people what just happened, and you will get as many answers as there are people. So reality is subjective. Is the wall in your room solid, or is it empty space? To me, it may appear solid. To a physicist with an electron microscope, it may be mostly empty space. Both perceptions are correct; both grids are useful.

The important thing about perception is that it can change, and it is relative to individuals, to time, to place, and to context. We can perceive ourselves as separate beings or as profoundly interconnected with everything around us. The more we experience ourselves as separate, the more we long for connection. We may seek connection in ways that are not productive, such as through drugs, alcohol, promiscuous sex, or damaging relationships. At other times, we may run from connection and fill our lives by being busy. None of these strategies help us discover the interconnectedness of all of life.

In Chapter Three, "Letting Go," I told you about *An American Tragedy,* by Theodore Dreiser, a novel in which a young man seeks the counsel of an Native American chief about his missing father. The chief is sitting on a woven rug. As part of his explanation of why such things happen, the chief asks the young man to turn over a corner of the rug. When he does, there lies a jumble of brightly colored threads. The chief points out that this is how the world looks to us. When the rug is turned right side up, thus showing the beautiful pattern, the chief suggests that this is how the world looks to God. The young man understands the relationship between the jumble and the pattern. Most often in our lives, however, we miss the relationship. Sometimes, and usually only much later, we see the interrelationships of those things that have shaped us. Wisdom is the ability to see the connection of all things.

In book two, verse twelve, of the *Bhagavad Gita,* Lord Krishna tells Arjuna that there is nothing but connection: *na tv evaham jatu nasam / na tvam neme janadhipah / na caiva bhavishyamah / sarve vayam atah param,* or "Verily, never was I not, were you not, or were these rulers not, nor will any one of us not be henceforth."[1] He reassures us that our connection with the Universe has existed, exists now, and will always exist. It transcends the cyclic existence of birth, and death, and time, and the natural laws of space. When we look inside ourselves for this connection, we will always find it. We are a reflection of it. When we can live with a deep faith in our connection to all that is, we fear less, want less, and need less.

One morning, I took my son to visit a new preschool to see if it was the right fit for him. I was eager to know how he felt about his experience. He was only three and one-half years old, so I tried to ask him in a way that I thought he could understand. I asked if his visit felt long or short. I thought if it felt long, it would probably mean that he was unhappy; if short, it might mean that he had had a good time. He said that it was neither: it was a circle. His answer reminded me that time and everything else is, indeed, a circle, and that all is included within it.

Whenever you feel afraid, anxious, lonely, or discouraged, you have forgotten that you are in the circle. To help you remember, there are practice suggestions at the end of this chapter that will help you to understand that you are critically important in the Universe. But first it is useful to know the difference between being special and being important. On the one hand, when we have the need to feel special, we want rules to change for us. We want to be first in line; we want to be the one for whom exceptions are made; and we want to be the one who doesn't die. This is a false sense of importance. On the other hand, each of us has a vital place in the scheme of things. Each of us has a *dharma*: a purpose, something to contribute to life. Perhaps happiness is the state that we feel when we find what it is that we can contribute with joy to the world.

When we embrace our importance, we are living our connection with others and the world around us. In this state, we can change the world. Just a kind gesture or a generous word can change another's day. Stopping to pay attention to what another person may need right now in her life and helping when appropriate can change that person's life. Connection is that process of knowing our importance to the Whole, as well as comprehending that others share this importance with us. When we do so, we are less likely to hate or fear. We can rest, secure in the knowledge that we are all eternal threads in the grand design.

Connection Practice

To help me remember that I am important, but not special, I say a Mantra for Daily Living: "Just happening." When I personalize what is happening as something that is being "done to me," I find myself reacting to the event and forgetting my interconnection with all of life. When I say the mantra, it is easier to remember that I am in the circle. Try it.

Other Practice Suggestions

- Pick up a piece of fruit that is in your fruit bowl or refrigerator. Just hold it. Where was it before you had it? In the grocery store? And before that? In a truck being delivered to market? And before that? In a fruit picker's box? Keep going. As you hold the apple or peach or plum or apricot, know that you are in the grand circle of people, places, and things that brought it to you, including the bus driver who dropped you off near the store. Without them, the peach could not be eaten. Without you, the peach could not be eaten.

- Take a walk. If possible, go barefoot for at least part of the time. Feel your connection to the grass or the sand beneath your feet.

- Sometimes we keep so busy that we forget our connection with others. Commit to a regular "time out" with your spouse or partner, children, or another family member. Make this time free from the business of your lives, away from telephones and fax machines and computers. Savor your time together.

- Take a yoga class. How wonderful: the opportunity to practice together.

- If you find yourself trying to make connection in unproductive ways, such as through drugs, alcohol, promiscuous sex, or damaging relationships, make a committment to reach out for help.

- Go to lunch with a friend.

Mantras for Daily Living
- I am in the circle.

- Just happening.

- I acknowledge the connection of all beings.

- People die, relationships don't.

- I choose to focus on my connection with you,
  not on what separates us.

18

Truth

satya-pratishthayam kriya-phala-ashrayatvam

When grounded in truthfulness, action and
its fruition depend on him.

—*Yoga Sutra* 2:36

In the *Yoga Sutra,* Patanjali lists *satya,* or "truth,"
as one of the most important practices for his students.
In book two, verse thirty-six, he acknowledges that there
is no way to move toward wholeness while caught up in
lies. He writes, *satya-pratishthayam kriya-phala-ashrayatvam,*
or "When grounded in truthfulness, action and its
fruition depend on him."[1] How do we achieve this truth?
We often lie, actively or tacitly, to avoid confronting ourselves and others, thus making our words and actions
anything but fruitful. We can begin with an examination
of Patanjali's sutra.

For Patanjali, truth has at least three levels. The first is
a basic communication that we seek in our daily lives, that is,
telling the truth about what we see, what we feel, and what we
need. And we want others to do the same for us. Although I
describe it as basic, it is not easy. What we see, feel, and need
is neither always clear to us nor always feels safe for us to
express. At these times, we may resort to telling "little white
lies," or lies of convenience. Some feel that these lies are benign
and do not hurt anyone: I disagree. I suffer just knowing that I've
told a lie, and all lies separate me from myself and from others.

The second level of satya is integrity. One day during the 1988 California drought, my then five-year-old daughter and I were taking a shower together to save water. She asked, "Mommy, what is integrity?" I struggled to answer her in a way that I thought that she could understand. I told her to imagine that she was walking through a park, and that she and several others saw a man drop a twenty dollar bill. Under these circumstances, if she returned the money to the man, that was honesty. But if no one else saw that the man had dropped the money and she still returned it, that was integrity. Integrity is internal honesty. It is telling the truth when no one would ever know. Integrity is refusing to tell a lie for self or for others.

The third level of truth has to do with the meaning of *satya* itself. *Sat* refers to the bedrock truth from which the Universe springs. It is the truth of God. *Ya* is an activating prefix in Sanskrit. Thus *satya* means "actively becoming the truth of the Universe."[2] I do not know about you, but I find this a daunting prospect.

I have a friend who says, "When in doubt, tell the truth." The irony, of course, is that we are always in doubt. We are in doubt about what actually is the truth in the first place. We are in doubt about what effect the truth will have on others and on ourselves. Finally, we are in doubt about our ability to withstand the possible effects of others knowing the truth. Yet we know somewhere deep inside that the truth is what everyone really wants most from us. And we know that the truth usually is exposed anyway. One of the most powerful understandings about truth that I have learned is that although telling or hearing the truth may help lift a weight from our shoulders, it may simultaneously break our hearts. Telling the truth is often not easy in the short run; it is, however, infinitely valuable in the long run.

To lie requires that you turn away from yourself and others, and this creates misery. Living satya is learning to make conscious choices about truthfulness in daily living. But telling the truth may smack of irritating righteousness without another important ingredient. Patanjali discusses *ahimsa,* or "nonharming," before satya. To me and to scholars with whom I have spoken, this means that truth cannot be practiced without ahimsa. For example, if you waltz into the room wearing what I think is the ugliest dress that I have ever seen and ask me how I like it, I am not practicing satya if I say that it is the ugliest dress that I have ever seen. The reason that my statement is not satya is that it does not express ahimsa first. I could say instead, "It fits you well." Or, if pressed, I could say that I did not like it. But in order to practice satya I must respond in a way that is not intended to harm. It is true that pain may be caused by my statements, but my intention is never to harm. I suggest that, before speaking or taking some other action, you first ask yourself these questions: Is it necessary? Is it true? Is it nonharming? If you can answer yes to all these questions, it may be okay to proceed. If not, you must weigh what is the right action in the situation.

Truthfulness includes the small things that no one but you would ever know about. I am sad to say that more than one yoga teacher has admitted to me that he lies about the income that he receives from teaching yoga in order to decrease the amount of money that he owes in taxes. I must admit that this is tempting. Like many yoga teachers, I receive a sizable portion of my income in cash, which could be difficult to trace. When I spoke to my husband about the possibility of not reporting this cash, his reply was straightforward: "We'll report every penny and sleep at night." I also realized that I could not lecture on truthfulness and clarity and, at the same time, lie about my income (or anything else). It is in the nitty-gritty details of your life that what I call "living your yoga" is all about.

I had another chance to learn about truthfulness in daily living when a friend asked me why I didn't have a radar detector in my van. I told her that if I used a one, I would be sending our children a message: It is okay to break the law (or lie) as long as you don't get caught. To do this, I would not be modeling integrity, so I reluctantly declined to purchase a radar detector. You may think that I am being too picky. However, if I want to live a truthful life that choice of truthfulness must be part of the decisions worth a penny as well as those worth a million dollars. And then there is telling yourself the truth in asana practice. How often do you coerce yourself into holding a pose longer than is beneficial? How often do you practice poses that are not appropriate? I suggest that we bring the same spirit of ahimsa and satya to every pose and to every practice.

In the verse cited previously, Patanjali is stating the results of becoming fully entrenched in the truth: You could not say anything that did not come true. In other words, if you are living the truth, then you cannot lie—because you are the truth. Everything you say comes true because you and the truth are one. Learning to speak from your place of truth is one of the most difficult—and one of the important things—that you can do in life. It is worth it, because it frees you from the separation that lying creates, and it simultaneously supports others in living and speaking their truths. This is what I want from myself, and this is what I want from those around me. Don't you?

Truth Practice

There is a simple exercise that you can try the next time that you are in a verbal conflict with someone. Try this *before* things start to heat up and you both lose it. As you begin to feel the conflict start, ask the following question: "What do you want from me right now?" This is a powerful question for several reasons. First, it acknowledges that the other person may not be getting what she wants and what she wants is important to you. Second, it focuses on "right now" and helps you both to let go of the past and what may have happened previously in the situation. And finally, by asking this question, you help the other person focus on her own truth: the truth of what she is feeling and needing. When you are able to do this, it is of great help not only to the other person but also to yourself. When you focus on the truth of right now, you are practicing in such a way as to truly live yoga.

Other Practice Suggestions

- Make a list of three things about which you lied. Forgive yourself. Silently ask those to whom you lied to forgive you, too.

- Ask your partner to tell you a truth that she has never before shared with you. Then do the same for her.

- Lying is a form of disrespecting self or others. The next time that you are tempted to tell a lie, even a little one, ask yourself whom you are disrespecting at that moment.

Mantras for Daily Living

- Is it true? Is it necessary? Is it nonharming?

- What do you want from me right now?

- When in doubt, tell the truth.

- Think the truth, tell the truth, and live the truth.

19

Success

bhogaishvarya-prasaktanam
  tayapahrita-cetasam
vyavasayatmika buddhih
  samadhau na vidhiyate

For those who are completely attached to enjoyment and
power, with the mind carried away by it—their wisdom faculty,
which is of the essence of will, is not settled in samadhi.

—*Bhagavad Gita* 2:44

Our culture is obsessed with success. We usually
measure it by achievement, such as winning at something or as
earning large sums of money. But it would seem that even
these significant accomplishments have drawbacks. Consider
the Olympics. Obviously, taking a medal in any event is the
zenith of athletic performance. However, although the winner
of the gold is often described as ecstatic, the silver medalist is
sometimes portrayed as disappointed. Even though her performance may have been clocked at only a few thousandths of a
second less than the gold medalist, she may feel like a failure.
This is the all-or-nothing philosophy of success. There is
another way of looking at life.

At five, my oldest child attended a ski camp. When
he returned from the mountains, he declared that he had
been in a race, and proudly displayed his second place medal.
When I asked him who else had been in the race, he said, "One
other boy and me." I instantly loved that camp for creating
an atmosphere that honored him for his participation. How

often do we consider that we have failed when we do not achieve what the world defines as success? Unfortunately, we tend to overlook the more meaningful measures of success in ourselves and others. Learning to have perspective about our successes and failures is vital.

The only real success in life is living with an open, loving heart. This allows you to connect with the Divine in yourself and in others. From this perspective, success can be seen in the choice of truth instead of lies, love instead of hate, and helping instead of turning away from the needs of others. If you honestly examine your life, you can find many examples of success. Perhaps you have raised loving children, or helped another human being in a time of need. Maybe you have risen above a difficult childhood to create a loving family of your own, or chosen, in a tense moment, silence instead of harsh speech. Perhaps you have learned to accommodate your own energy level, getting help when your workload is too great or relinquishing being on the A list, rather than putting health and happiness at risk.

The yoga tradition counsels us about success in the *Bhagavad Gita*, book two, verse forty-four: *bhogaishvarya-prasaktanam / tayapahrita-cetasam / vyavasayatmika buddhih / samadhau na vidhiyate*, or "For those who are completely attached to enjoyment and power, with the mind carried away by it—their wisdom faculty, which is of the essence of will, is not settled in samadhi."[1] In this verse, Krishna explains the nature of success, emphasizing that all those things that are obtained in the world are transitory and are not ultimately success. When we define success in a worldly way, we not only limit ourselves and those around us, but we also contribute to our false perception of reality. In simpler terms, we are missing out on life. There is no substitute for peace. Even though we pay lip service to it, we forget this fact on a daily basis. One way to remember it is to enjoy the simplest of pleasures: the color of a rose, the softness of the wind on your skin, the laughter of a passing stranger—or coming in second out of two in a ski race.

Am I suggesting that we give up and no longer try to achieve our goals? Absolutely not. It is not the possession of accomplishments that is the problem: rather, the problem is the belief that they are the solution to an aching soul. When my children were young, I asked them for lists of what they wanted for Christmas. (Of course, Santa edited these to exclude some dramatic requests, such as a giraffe!) I tried to buy the exact gifts that my children requested. I strove to give my children what they longed for because I wanted them to realize that they could have the material things that seemed so important and still be unhappy. If they never got what they wanted, it would be easy to blame their unhappiness on that. I reasoned that if my kids received the gifts they wanted (again, within limits), they would have a better chance of learning to find satisfaction other than in material goods. As my children matured, they began to ask for gifts that could not be found in a store.

The question, then, is, how can we enjoy our worldly successes and yet not identify ourselves with them? When it comes to our approach to success, we are like a tightrope walker. After all, it does not matter whether she falls to the left or to the right: in either case, she has fallen. In the same way, if we think that success is the solution to our lives and put too much emphasis on it, then we fall to the left. However, if we ignore the material gifts that we have been given, we fall to the right because we miss out on great enjoyment in the world. Finding the balance between these two extremes is how I would define success.

Success Practice

To help get perspective on the all-or-nothing philosophy of success, make a list of your successes and failures in the past six months. Were there any successes embedded in your failures? Were there any failures embedded in your successes? Can you see how there is some of both in both?

Other Practice Suggestions

- Are you so invested in being seen as successful that you hold on to things longer than is good for you? Is it time to resign from a committee or a job, or give up a hobby grown stale? Can you do so without resentment and in a way that does not harm you or anyone else?

- The next time you play a game, whether it is cards or tennis, do not keep score. Focus on the success of enjoying the game, not winning.

- Ask someone who knows you well to share with you what they see as your biggest success in life. You might be surprised.

- Keep a success journal. Every night, spend two minutes writing down at least one success you had that day: perhaps you smiled at someone who was grumpy, picked up trash that someone else had dropped, or remembered your mother's birthday. Once in a while, leaf through the pages, and enjoy all the little successes that make up the fabric of your life.

Mantras for Daily Living

- I acknowledge my successes.

- I live in balance.

- I am willing to enjoy life.

- Coming in second is a success.

- A successful life is one lived in friendship and love.

- Love, not wealth, is success.

20

Nonviolence

ahimsa-pratishthayam tat-samnidhau vaira-tyagah

When the *yogin* is grounded in the virtue of non-harming, all enmity is abandoned in his presence.

—*Yoga Sutra* 2:35

One day, my young daughter asked me if I had ever killed anyone. My first reaction was disbelief. Then, because I always try to answer my kids' questions honestly, I said that I had never killed anyone. But my answer made me think. It is true that I had not knowingly killed anyone, but I did not actually *know* that my actions had not generated a ripple-in-the-pond effect that had caused harm, even death. I looked down at the Oriental rug in my living room. Could I honestly say that there was no child labor involved? Could I honestly say that my economic choices had not caused misery or death for someone in a distant country? Perhaps my offhanded rudeness during driving one day had affected another driver's mood so that she had later acted with anger and thus an accident had happened. The question of how our choices may harm others is a complicated one.

In book two, verse thirty, of the *Yoga Sutra*, Patanjali lists five *yama*, or "restraints," that he suggests yoga students follow in order to move toward wholeness.[1] The first of these is *ahimsa*, which comes from two words: *a*, meaning "not," and *himsa*, meaning "harm." Thus, *ahimsa* means "nonharming." Patanjali says that we are to actively practice nonharming as the foundation of practice. But what does this mean in our daily lives?

The most effective way to practice ahimsa is to pay attention to our angry and violent thoughts. If we are being honest, we can admit that we have these kinds of thoughts daily. Usually, we feel that all is well because we choose not to act on them. Society's very existence depends upon the separation between thought and action. If we acted out all of our thoughts, society would not exist. However, if we are committed to personal evolution, then we must deepen our understanding of our responsibility. When we have an angry or violent thought, it is significant, because thoughts are the foundation for our words and our actions. If we want to change the way that we interact with the world, then we have to change our words and actions by changing our thoughts.

This change comes first and foremost from the process of paying meticulous attention to a thought. When we do, we have a greater chance of separating from it, a process that I call disidentification. This means that we may continue to have the thought but realize that it is only a thought, that is, a neurological-biochemical event: It is not who we are.

One thought or attitude that can be the genesis of angry or violent thoughts is the root thought, I am special. As discussed in Chapter Seventeen, "Connection," we all want to be special and not have to follow the rules. We want to be able to break the speed limit, or to move to the front of the line, or to ignore a deadline. This wish separates us from others, and provides a background for us to think of others as objects to manipulate in order to get what we want. When we think of others as objects, it is easier to injure them through thoughts, words, and deeds.

Remember, we are all critically important to the Universe. Each of us has something to offer and something to receive. Our words and our actions have the potential to affect everyone and everything around us. To recognize our own importance requires our recognizing the importance of others. When we do, we treat them with respect and, therefore, practice ahimsa.

In book two, verse thirty-five, of the *Yoga Sutra,* Patanjali states, *ahimsa-pratishthayam tat-samnidhau vaira-tyagah,* or "When the *yogin* is grounded in the virtue of non-harming, all enmity is abandoned in his presence."[2] Here he paints a picture of what happens as we perfect nonharming in our lives. As we begin to live the teaching of ahimsa, those around us give up their hostility. What a gift to the world! As we watch our thoughts, and through that observation allow for some distance between us and them, we move further away from having violent thoughts in the first place. And as these habitual thoughts leave our consciousness, a change happens in us and all around us. There is power in this practice, and each of us is integral to the creation of nonharming.

We must, however, be clear about the difference between acting with violence and acting in a way that protects self and others. There is a story about ahimsa that I've been told by many teachers throughout the years. A certain *sadhu,* or "wandering monk," would make a yearly teaching visit to some villages. One year, as he entered a village, he saw a large, menacing snake terrorizing the people. The sadhu spoke to the snake and taught him about ahimsa. When the sadhu made his next annual visit, he saw the snake. This once magnificent creature was skinny and bruised. The sadhu asked the snake what had happened. The snake replied that he had taken the teaching of ahimsa to heart and had stopped terrorizing the village. But because he was no longer menacing, the children now taunted him and threw rocks at him, and he was afraid to leave his hiding place. The sadhu shook his head. "I *did* advise against violence," he said to the snake, "but I never told you not to *hiss.*"

We all want a world that is peaceful and safe, and we sometimes feel overwhelmed when we see the hatred, anger, and violence around us. I am reminded of a flier advertising "A Vision of Global Peace," a workshop with Marshall B. Rosenberg, about whom I wrote in Chapter Nine, "Control." The flier quoted Dr. Rosenberg: "Violence in any form is a tragic expression of our unmet needs."[3] I agree with Dr. Rosenberg. I would add that there is hope. Learning to observe and eventually let go of our own violent thoughts is the catalyst for change that the world so desperately needs. One mind letting go of violence is one mind not contributing to suffering in the world. And reducing suffering is the ultimate intention of the practice of ahimsa.

Nonviolence Practice

At the end of my yoga classes, I ring bells to signify to my students that our time together has come to an end, and to gradually bring them back from relaxation to normal consciousness. My students tell me that the sound of the bells holds various meanings for them: for example, one thing is ending; another thing is beginning. You can use the sound of bells around you to remind you of your dedication to a life of nonviolence. There is the sound of a telephone, a church bell, your yoga timer, your beeper watch, a percussion instrument in a piece of music, and a noon lunch whistle. Each time that you hear a bell, say to yourself, I dedicate myself to nonviolence.

Other Practice Suggestions

- If you have your own bells, ring them at the beginning and end of your yoga or meditation practice to symbolize your dedication of your practice time to nonviolence. If you do not have bells, use something around your house, such as a spoon struck against a crystal glass or vase.

- Inspire yourself to practice nonviolence. There are modern-day examples of those who have dedicated their lives to ahimsa, such as Martin Luther King Jr., Thich Nhat Hanh, Mother Theresa, and Mahatma Gandhi. Read their biographies or books written by them to learn about their journey to living in peace.

- The next time that you notice that you have lashed out at someone, replay the scene in your head. This time, practice ahimsa.

- Pay particular attention to your yoga and *pranayama* practice. Can you practice nonviolence toward yourself by doing less and being more?

- For just one day, silently remind yourself of ahimsa just before you speak.

Mantras for Daily Living

- I am peace.

- I make a commitment to practicing yoga poses with ahimsa.

- I choose to respond with equanimity.

- My intention today is to invite peace into all of my words and actions.

21

Love

yadriccha-labha-samtushto
dvandvatito vimatsarah
samah siddhav asiddau ca
kritvapi na nibadhyate

Content with what is chance-obtained, transcending the
opposites, without envy, the same in success and failure,
though performing actions—he is not bound.

—*Bhagavad Gita 4:22*

Ask most people and they would probably confirm
that love was the most important thing in their lives and the
last thing that they would be willing to give up. Most of us
would probably choose a short life filled with love than a long
one lived without it. Yet we would be hard pressed to find a
word with more connotations and denotations than *love*. It
seems to cover everything from a brief, lustful romance to an
enduring relationship.

I remember the first time that my heart was broken
by love. I was a teenager and a boy dumped me for someone else. I was convinced that my life was over. I continued
to carry a torch for him for a long time: it must have been
two weeks before I developed a crush on someone new! At
the time, I thought that the love that I had felt for the boy
who had dumped me was wasted love. Now, well beyond
my teens, I feel that there is no such thing as wasted love.
Any love that we experience holds great power, that is, the
power to transform both us and those whom we love. In

fact, *without* love we cannot be transformed.

Sometimes I notice my yoga students practicing their less than favorite poses with a ho-hum attitude. At these moments, I remind them that although yoga is powerful, it cannot transform us unless we love it. When we love, we are receptive to the "other." When we love, we are vulnerable. Although being vulnerable can be frightening, it is also the doorway to the ultimate freedom written about in book four, verse twenty-two, of the *Bhagavad Gita: yadriccha-labha-samtushto / dvandvatito vimatsarah / samah siddhav asiddau ca / kritvapi na nibadhyate,* or "Content with what is chance-obtained, transcending the opposites, without envy, the same in success and failure, though performing actions—he is not bound."[1]

Here, Krishna explains what life is like when you are not bound by the attraction of opposites, and that when this state is experienced, there is no reaction to the vicissitudes of life. When you react, you are not in a state of love. When you can love without expectation, you are in a state of pure love. Mostly, what is declared to be love is not. Rather, it is need, or fear, or the desire for power over another person. Love in its purest sense is not based upon what you get from the relationship, but on what the relationship allows you to give. The depth of your love is not reflected in what the other makes you feel, but in your willingness to give of yourself. Love's job is to lead you to intimacy with what is enduring in yourself and in others. Whether this connection lasts for seconds or for decades, love is not wasted. Through it, you have been transformed.

A word of caution: I am not recommending that you accept the actions of others, even those whom you love, without discrimination. For example, I suggest to my students that when they study with a yoga teacher, including me, they imagine taking an invisible, finely woven net to class. I counsel them to let only those things pass through the net that are life affirming. Finally, I say that even if the teacher were Patanjali himself, you should never discard the net. It is a reminder of your obligation to yourself to be discriminating. Without it, you may miss the opportunity to love yourself.

I learned this lesson in an interesting way. One day after teaching my yoga class, I was feeling particularly connected to the Universe. I was in love with everyone. I boarded the streetcar, bound for home. After I had been seated for only a few minutes, a drunk man staggered down the aisle, stopped, leaned over me, and began to verbally harass me. I thought to myself that God must be saying, You think that you love everyone? Watch this. As the man continued to sway back and forth and talk loudly, I consciously closed down my energy. He instantly left me alone. I learned a powerful lesson that day. When you open up your heart, it can be out of pride. Had I been wiser, I would have realized that it would be better if I kept my energy to myself unless I was truly the loving person that I thought I was. Vulnerability is not an excuse for forgetting to honor the appropriateness of sharing love. Learning to share the deep opening of your heart is life's most important lesson. But it needs discrimination as its partner.

I learned another valuable lesson about love from a friend and yoga teacher who died a few years ago. We both had always been fascinated with graveyards, and used to take walks in one near her house. We would occasionally discuss our own deaths, and promised each other that whoever died first would try to contact the other. I forgot about this promise. But in a quiet moment a few days after her death, I heard her wonderful and distinctive laugh. The sound was so clear that I actually jumped, startled by the nearness of the sound. How are you?, I thought. She answered me not in words but with what felt like a thought injected into my brain. She said that she was fine and that it was wonderful on the other side. Most important, she communicated that the only thing I was to do while living was to love everyone. This, she let me know, is the purpose of life. The experience sent chills up my spine and over my scalp. It left me both shaken and reassured. I am grateful for my friendship or my unconscious mind, whatever was the genesis of this experience. It reminded me of what is the only important thing in life: sharing the connection we call love.

Love Practice

Language can be limiting. The words "I love you" sometimes do not really express what you want to say. Try this practice. The next time that you are aware that you are feeling love, say, "I am having loving feelings toward you right now." This statement does two things: it acknowledges the feelings and it focuses on the moment.

When you say "I love you," it implies that there is something about your love that is dependent on the other person and her behavior. In reality, love is the choice that you make when you are able to connect with her beyond your ego. Saying "I am having loving feelings" focuses on what spontaneously arises in you at that very moment. And this remembering to focus on the moment is the heart of living your yoga.

Other Practice Suggestions

- Think about a situation in which you thought you were in love. How could that situation have been different if you had brought love's partner—discrimination—along for the ride?

- The next time that you go to your yoga class, take your invisible net with you. Notice how discrimination affects your experience of the teacher and the poses. (Actually, I recommend that you take your invisible net of discrimination with you everywhere.)

- Make a list of those things that inspire feelings of love: a sunset, a blooming daffodil, your cat, the ocean, a painting, watching your sleeping child, preparing food for your family, or seeing a friend. Take time out to deeply experience one each week. Notice your feelings of connection.

Mantras for Daily Living

- I open to giving and receiving love.

- Love dispels fear.

- I am having loving feelings toward myself right now.

- I am having loving feelings toward you right now.

- Love is connection with myself.

- Love is life's attempt to tell me that there is always hope.

- When I love, I am living yoga.

Notes

Introduction

1. An unpublished study conducted in 1999 by *Yoga Journal*, Berkeley, Calif.

2. Adapted from Georg Feuerstein, *The Yoga-Sutra of Patanjali: A New Translation and Commentary* (Rochester, Vt.: Inner Traditions, 1989), 80–82.

3. Dag Hammarskjöld, *Markings* (New York: Alfred A. Knopf, Inc., 1964), xxi.

Chapter 1

Epigraph: Feuerstein, *Yoga-Sutra*, 28.

1. Ibid.

2. Ibid., author's translation.

3. Author's translation.

Chapter 2

Epigraph: Feuerstein, *Yoga-Sutra*, 34.

1. Scott Peck, *The Road Less Traveled: A New Psychology of Love, Traditional Values, and Spiritual Growth* (New York: Simon and Schuster, 1978), 15.

2. Feuerstein, *Yoga-Sutra*, 34.

3. Ibid.

Chapter 3

Epigraph: Feuerstein, *Yoga-Sutra*, 34.

1. Ibid.

2. Ibid.

3. Author's translation.

4. Feuerstein, *Yoga-Sutra*, 61–62.

5. Author's translation.

6. Ibid.

7. Feuerstein, *Yoga-Sutra,* 61.

Chapter 4

Epigraph: Feuerstein, *Yoga-Sutra,* 90.

1. Ibid.

2. Ibid.

3. Author's translation.

4. Author's definition.

Chapter 5

Epigraph: Feuerstein, *Yoga-Sutra,* 40. Author's translation.

1. Ibid.

2. *A Zen Harvest: Japanese Folk Zen Sayings,* comp. and trans. Sôiku Shigematsu (Berkeley, Calif.: North Point Press, 1988), 95.

3. Ibid., 19.

Chapter 6

Epigraph: Feuerstein, *Yoga-Sutra,* 76.

1. Ibid.

Chapter 7

Epigraph: Georg Feuerstein, *The Bhagavad-Gita: Yoga of Contemplation and Action* (New Delhi: Arnold-Heinemann, 1980), 61.

1. Ibid.

Chapter 8

Epigraph: Feuerstein, *Yoga-Sutra,* 47–48.

1. Ibid., 80.

2. Ibid., 47–48.

3. *Webster's Ninth New Collegiate Dictionary,* s.v. "compassion"; and ibid., s.v. "com-."

Chapter 9

Epigraph: Feuerstein, *Yoga-Sutra,* 36.

1. Hammarskjöld, *Markings,* 8.

2. Feuerstein, *Yoga-Sutra,* 36.

3. Suzuki Roshi, quoted in Les Kaye, *Zen at Work: A Zen Teacher's 30-Year Journey in Corporate America* (New York: Crown, 1996), 42.

4. Marshall B. Rosenberg, at a workshop on nonviolent communication (San Francisco, Calif., 29 May 1997). For information about Dr. Rosenberg's work, contact The Center for Nonviolent Communication, P.O. Box 2662, Sherman, TX 75091; 903/893–3886. For information about his book, *Nonviolent Communication: A Language of Compassion,* contact PuddleDancer Press, P.O. Box 1204, Del Mar, CA 92014; 877/367–2849.

Chapter 10

Epigraph: Feuerstein, *Bhagavad-Gita,* 54–55.

1. Ibid.

2. Kathy Weston, R.N., telephone conversation with author, 1 April 1999.

3. Feuerstein, *Yoga-Sutra,* 64–65.

4. Weston, telephone conversation.

Chapter 11

Epigraph: Feuerstein, *Yoga-Sutra,* 55. Author's translation.

1. Feuerstein, *Yoga-Sutra,* 55.

2. Author's translation.

3. Author's translation.

4. Feuerstein, *Yoga-Sutra,* 47–48.

5. Gay Hendricks, *The Ten Second Miracle: Creating Relationship Breakthroughs* (San Francisco: HarperSanFrancisco, 1998), 41.

Chapter 12

Epigraph: Feuerstein, *Yoga-Sutra,* 64.

1. CALVIN AND HOBBES; copyright © Watterson. Reprinted with permission of UNIVERSAL PRESS SYNDICATE. All rights reserved.

2. Feuerstein, *Yoga-Sutra,* 64.

3. Author's translation.

4. Ibid.

Chapter 13

Epigraph: Feuerstein, *Yoga-Sutra,* 69–70.

1. Arthur C. Guyton, M.D., *Basic Human Physiology: Normal Function and Mechanisms of Disease* (Philadelphia: W.B. Saunders Company, 1971), 515.

2. Feuerstein, *Yoga-Sutra,* 69–70.

3. Ibid., 63.

4. Ibid., 62.

Chapter 14

Epigraph: Feuerstein, *Yoga-Sutra,* 63.

1. Ibid.

2. Shakyamuni Buddha, quoted in Thich Nhat Hanh, *Plum Village Chanting Book* (Berkeley, Calif.: Parallax Press, 1991), 131.

3. Ibid.

4. Ibid.

Chapter 15

Epigraph: Feuerstein, *Bhagavad-Gita*, 88.

1. Feuerstein, *Yoga-Sutra*, 80.

2. Ibid., 79–80.

3. Ibid., 80.

4. Ibid., 86.

5. Feuerstein, *Bhagavad-Gita*, 88.

6. Feuerstein, *Yoga-Sutra*, 88.

Chapter 16

Epigraph: Feuerstein, *Bhagavad-Gita*, 73.
1. Ibid.

Chapter 17

Epigraph: Feuerstein, *Bhagavad-Gita*, 60.
1. Ibid.

Chapter 18

Epigraph: Feuerstein, *Yoga Sutra*, 85.
1. Ibid.
2. Author's translation.

Chapter 19

Epigraph: Feuerstein, *Bhagavad-Gita*, 63.
1. Ibid.

Chapter 20

Epigraph: Feuerstein, *Yoga-Sutra*, 84.
1. Ibid., 80.
2. Ibid., 84.

3. For information about Dr. Rosenberg's work, see Chapter Nine, note 4.

Chapter 21

Epigraph: Feuerstein, *Bhagavad-Gita*, 81.

1. Ibid.

Appreciations

Grateful acknowledgment is made to the following for permission to reprint previously published material:

Farrar, Straus and Giroux: Excerpts #81 and #447 from *A Zen Harvest: Japanese Folk Zen Sayings,* compiled and translated by Sôiku Shigematsu; copyright © 1988 by Sôiku Shigematsu. Reprinted with permission of North Point Press, a division of FARRAR, STRAUS AND GIROUX, LLC. All rights reserved.

Georg Feuerstein: Excerpts from *The Bhagavad-Gita: Yoga of Contemplation and Action* by Georg Feuerstein; copyright © 1980 by Georg Feuerstein. Reprinted with permission of GEORG FEUERSTEIN. All rights reserved.

Inner Traditions International: Excerpts from *The Yoga-Sutra of Patanjali: A New Translation and Commentary* by Georg Feuerstein; copyright © 1979, 1989 by Georg Feuerstein. Reprinted with permission of INNER TRADITIONS INTERNATIONAL, Rochester, VT 05767. All rights reserved.

Parallax Press: Excerpt from the *Plum Village Chanting Book* by Thich Nhat Hanh; copyright © 1991 by Eglise Bouddhique Unifiée. Reprinted with permission of PARALLAX PRESS, Berkeley, CA 94707. All rights reserved.

Universal Press Syndicate: CALVIN AND HOBBES; copyright © by Watterson. Reprinted with permission of UNIVERSAL PRESS SYNDICATE. All rights reserved.

Yoga Journal: Statistic from an unpublished study conducted in 1999. Reprinted with permission of YOGA JOURNAL, Berkeley, Calif. All rights reserved.

In addition, much appreciation goes to

Richard Eskite/San Francisco: For his photograph of the author on the back cover.

Georg Feuerstein: For his personal help with transliterating Sanskrit.

About the Author

Judith Lasater has taught yoga since 1971. She holds a doctorate in East-West psychology and is a physical therapist. Judith is president of the California Yoga Teachers Association, and serves on the advisory boards of *Yoga Journal* and the Yoga Research and Education Center.

Her yoga training includes study with B.K.S. Iyengar in India and the United States. She teaches ongoing yoga classes and trains yoga teachers in kinesiology, yoga therapeutics, and the *Yoga Sutra* at the Iyengar Yoga Institute of San Francisco. Judith also gives workshops throughout the United States, and has taught in Canada, England, France, Indonesia, Japan, Mexico, Peru, and Russia.

She writes extensively on the therapeutic aspects of yoga. Her best-selling *Relax and Renew: Restful Yoga for Stressful Times* (Rodmell Press) is the first book exclusively devoted to the supported yoga poses and breathing techniques that make up restorative yoga.

Her popular "Asana" column ran in *Yoga Journal* for thirteen years, and she continues to contribute articles on a variety of subjects. In addition, her writing has appeared in numerous magazines and books, including *Yoga International, Natural Health, Sports Illustrated for Women, Prevention, Alternative Therapies, Numedx, International Journal of Yoga Therapy* (formerly *The Journal of the International Association of Yoga Therapists*), *Complementary Therapies in Rehabilitation* (Slack), *Living Yoga* (Jeremy P. Tarcher/Perigee), *American Yoga* (Grove Press), *The New*

Yoga for People Over 50 (Health Communications), and *Lilias, Yoga, and Your Life* (Macmillan).

Judith Lasater lives in the San Francisco Bay Area with her husband and three children.

Yoga with Judith Lasater, Ph.D., P.T.

There are several ways to study yoga with Judith Lasater. Whether you are looking for the camaraderie of a class, the guidance of a book, or a yoga vacation, these resources will support your practice.

Yoga Classes, Vacations, Workshops, and Seminars:

Judith Lasater teaches ongoing yoga classes, leads yoga vacations, and offers special workshops and seminars, including Relax and Renew Seminars® and Living Your Yoga Seminars®. All are open to individuals, yoga teachers, and health care professionals. See www.judithlasater.com for the author's teaching schedule.

Book: *Relax and Renew: Restful Yoga for Stressful Times* (Berkeley, Calif.: Rodmell Press, 1995). Experience the *rest* of your life with restorative yoga, the supported poses and breathing techniques that help to ease the effects of stress. Includes programs for back pain, headaches, insomnia, jet lag, breathing problems, menstruation, pregnancy, and menopause. Softcover; 240 pages; more than one hundred photographs, charts, and illustrations; $21.95 (plus s/h and state tax in California).

Booklet: *Yoga for Pregnancy: A* Yoga Journal *Reprint* (Berkeley, Calif.: Yoga Journal, 1994). Yoga poses and breathing exercises to help you stay flexible and healthy during pregnancy and the postpartum period. Booklet, twelve pages, thirteen photographs; $2.50 (plus s/h and state tax in California).

To order or for more information: Contact Rodmell Press at 2147 Blake St., Berkeley, CA 94704–2715; 800/841–3123 or 510/841–3123; 510/841–3191 (fax); RodmellPrs@aol.com (e-mail).

About the Illustrator

Gracing the front and back covers of *Living Your Yoga* is *California Poppies,* by artist and yoga student Andie Thrams. The original lithograph (copyright © 1985, 11″ x 25″) was inspired, like most of her work, by drawings and color studies done in the field.

Born in Northern California, Andie divides her time between Berkeley, California, and Bird Creek, Alaska, a small town at the foot of the Chugach Mountains, on Cook Inlet. She has a bachelor's degree in art practice from the University of California at Berkeley, and continues to study painting and printmaking with various teachers.

Andie has published her images as notecards and posters since 1980, when she founded Larkspur Graphics. At the heart of her work is a lifelong fascination with the colors, forms, and patterns found in the natural world, especially plants.

In 1983, she began her study of yoga in the style of B.K.S. Iyengar with Lynne Minton, director of Yoga, The Inner Dance, in Anchorage, Alaska. For Andie, drawing and painting are spiritual practices. "They are very much like yoga," she says. "Each cultivates openness and stillness: in the eyes and the mind, in the body and the heart."

For more information about Andie Thrams and her paintings, posters, and notecards, contact Larkspur Graphics, 1407 Eleventh Ave., Seattle, WA 98122; 800/779–4303.

From the Publisher

Rodmell Press publishes books and tapes on yoga and Buddhism. In the *Bhagavad Gita* it is written, "Yoga is skill in action." It is our hope that these products will help individuals develop a more skillful practice—one that brings peace to their daily lives and to the Earth.

We thank all those whose support, encouragement, and practical advice sustain us in our efforts. In particular, we are grateful to Reb Anderson, B. K. S. Iyengar, and Yvonne Rand for their inspiration.

For a copy of our catalog and to receive information on future titles, contact us at

Rodmell Press
2147 Blake St.
Berkeley, CA 94704–2715
510/841–3123 or 800/841–3123
510/841–3191 (fax)
RodmellPrs@aol.com (e-mail)

Rodmell Press titles are available to the trade from the following distributors:

North America

SCB Distributors
15608 S. New Century Dr.
Gardena, CA 90248–2129
United States of America
310/532–9400 or 800/729–6423
310/532–7001 (fax)
info@scbdistributors.com (e-mail)

Australia/New Zealand

Boobook Publications

P.O. Box 163

Tea Gardens, NSW 2324

Australia

+61–49–970811

+61–49–971089 (fax)

boobook@compuserve.com (e-mail)

United Kingdom/Europe

Wisdom Books

25 Stanley Road

Ilford, Essex IG1 1RW

United Kingdom

+44–(0)–208–553–5020

+44–(0)–208–553–5122 (fax)

sales@wisdombooks.org (e-mail)